MW01134941

The Best Guide Ever to
PALM SPRINGS
CELEBRITY HOMES

Even though this book is
The Best Guide Ever to Palm Springs Celebrity Homes,
it is far from complete.

If you see room for improvement and would like to share a
story or rumor regarding a Palm Springs celebrity; or if you
simply want to inform me of a typo, send an email to
MeeksEric@hotmail.com.

And if you really like the book,
please post a review on your favorite book website for me.

Thank you,
Eric G. Meeks

This book is brought to you by the
Wrubleski Meeks Team

Long-time Palm Springs resident, Eric G. Meeks and, Canadian ex-Pat, Tracey Wrubleski Meeks spear-head The Wrubleski Meeks Team, specializing in Palm Springs area real estate. With over twenty years experience in real estate and more than thirty five years in the desert, they can quickly answer any and all primary and secondary home ownership, property listing, real estate purchase and rental questions. Known for incredible knowledge, honesty and maximizing dollar values, Eric and Tracey look forward to helping others seeking to take advantage of the very unique opportunities in the Palm Springs real estate market.

The Works of Eric G. Meeks

Fiction
The Author Murders
Witch of Tahquitz
Six Stories

Non-Fiction
Intuitive Reflections: The Art of Ron Klotchman
The Best Guide Ever to Palm Springs Celebrity Homes
Lawrence Welk's First Television Champagne Lady Roberta Linn
PS I Love Lucy: The Story of Lucille Ball in Palm Springs
Not Now Lord, I've Got Too Much to Do
A Brief History of Copyright Law
Reversing Discrimination

Short Stories
Apollo Thorn: Moons of Jupiter: Corporate Wars
Mirth the Dragon vs the Book Dealer Knight
Selling Space Share
Vampire Dreams

Edited by Eric G. Meeks
1853 Cavalry Quest for a Southwest Railroad Route

Websites
https://www.facebook.com/eric.g.meeks
http://www.flickr.com/photos/ericgmeeks/
http://ezinearticles.com/?expert=Eric_G._Meeks
http://www.youtube.com/user/meekseric?ob=0&feature=results_main
http://www.PSCelebrityHomes.com

Facts and Legends of the Village of Palm Springs

The Best Guide Ever to
PALM SPRINGS
CELEBRITY HOMES

ERIC G. MEEKS

MeeksEric@hotmail.com

Horatio Limburger Oglethorpe, Publisher

The Best Guide Ever to Palm Springs Celebrity Homes
© 2012 by Horatio Limburger Oglethorpe, Publisher

ISBN-13: 978-1479328598
ISBN-10: 1479328596

First Printing

Updated: 10-17-2013

Most photos were taken by Eric G. Meeks himself.
For a complete list of photo sources,
please see the bibliography at the end of the book.

Printed in the Unites States of America

For all my old Palm Springs High School friends,
Class of 1983, and other Palm Springs friends made throughout the years, many of whom helped create this book with stories of their youth and their personal encounters with
celebrities over their lifetimes.

And for my Dad, Gaylon Darrell Meeks Sr., (deceased),
who originally thought of the series
Facts and Legends of the Village of Palm Springs.
He would have enjoyed helping piece together all the unique
stories and history of the town I (we) love.

Thank you,
EGM

Arner Saml D (Desert Realty Co) h68-615 Broadway CC box 228 48-3251
Arnez Desi (Lucille B) actor h334 Hermosa pl
Arnholz Walter Mrs r1563 S Palm Canyon dr

From the 1954 Palm Springs Phone Directory.

Farrell Albt J (Edna) h1550 Riverside dr—North 47502
FARRELL CHARLES D (Virginia Valli) Pres Racquet Club, h630 Tachevah Dr, 52345
Farrell David (Gladys M) r788 N Palm Canyon dr 49095

From the 1954 Palm Springs Phone Directory.

Freund Wm F (Pearl) (Del Pico Lodge) r Los Angeles
Frey Albt (Clark & Frey) h1150 Paseo El Mirador
Friedberg Saml (Betty T) h710 Paseo Anza 46445

From the 1951 Palm Springs Phone Directory.

Hoover H Earl (Dorothy) h Smoke Tree Ranch 48031
Hope Bob (Dolores) actor h1188 E El Alameda
Hopkins C Harold (Louise C) archt h416 S Patencio rd 47941

From the 1947 Palm Springs Phone Directory.

SIMSARIAN HENRY A (L Pauline) Plumbing—Heating—Cooling 850 N Palm Canyon
dr 47414
Sinatra Frank (Nancy) h1147 E Alejo
Singer David (Esther) apts 330 Sepulveda rd

From the 1947 Palm Springs Phone Directory.

TABLE OF CONTENTS

How I Know What I Know   10
1. Little Tuscany   13
2. Racquet Club   29
3. Racquet Club Estates   41
4. Desert Park Estates   63
5. Las Palmas   69
6. Movie Colony & El Mirador   139
7. Central PS: Sunrise to Airport   189
8. Tennis Club   195
9. Central PS: Warm Sands   215
10. Central PS: Sunmor   227
11. Demuth Park   241
12. Deep Well   247
13. Mesa   279
14. South PS: Smoke Tree   305
15. South PS: Canyon CC & Twin Palms   311
16. Andreas Hills   339
17. Araby, Los Compadres & Southridge   347
18. Seven Lakes   361
19. Golf Club Estates   371
Down Valley Addresses   375
Unverified Addresses   384
Special Thanks   389
Research Sources   390
Index   393

How I Know What I Know

I hope this book starts some good conversations. This book is appropriately named. It is the Best Guide Ever to Palm Springs Celebrity Homes. But, it is far from complete. It is merely the Best Guide Ever, so far. I don't consider my work here done. As you peruse these pages and hopefully are fascinated at the depth of information I've been able to gather, please consider that there is a lot more I hope to do and I want your help.

You'll find my email address under my name on the title page. If, when you read this book, you would like to share your own celebrity story and see it in print I want you to email me so I can include it in future editions. In this way, we'll make a second edition and eventually a third edition, and more, as the information gets more and more compiled and more and more exact.

You'll notice with some of the homes I openly state that a celebrities rumor of residence might not be verifiable. In some cases that means exactly what it says. I simply could not verify, yet, that a celebrity slept there or rented there or visited there. These things do not always leave a paper trail. There was no rental agreement, lease, other authors work, newspaper article, magazine reporting, radio transcript, etc., to validate the claim. It is therefore simply unverifiable even if it is strongly believed to be true. In a few cases my investigations revealed the claims to be absolutely false and I openly state this.

In many more cases, I think there'll be Palm Springs homeowners who will be pleasantly surprised to find their home has a celebrity heritage that heretofore was unknown to them.

Many people may wonder how I'm able to comfortably make the claims I do in this book. I mean most of this material is about Hollywood people, some of which I never met and many of which were dead before I was born.

So, here's the truth: I've lived in Palm Springs since 1976 and over the last 35+ years my parents and I have owned several very unique businesses which gave us access to a lot of the celebrities.

In 1980, my parents opened The Bookstore & More in Rancho Mirage. One of the unique features of this store was that it had the most centrally located Western Union in the desert. In the days before the internet, Western Union was the most viable way to send personal messages and money. I personally delivered messages to Ronald Reagan, Tony Curtis, Ozzy Osborne, and more. In the wee early morning hours, my father delivered the New York Times newspaper. His personal rolodex would make you whistle with glee at the list of celebrities. Again, in the pre-internet days (and many would argue that what I'm about to say is still true, myself included) the NY Times was the best national source of news in the country. Anybody who was anybody who cared about the national spotlight: business people, politicians, celebrities, etc., ordered the NY Times from my Dad. Author Harold Robbins would pay his paper bill by allowing me to come over to his house with a boxful of books which he would sign for me in person.

During the 1990's, I owned my own very special, very fun business, called Celebrity Books.com, which was both a brick and mortar bookstore and a website which dealt primarily in autographed books and memorabilia and brought more celebrities to Palm Springs than just about any other organization, except for maybe the PS Film Fest; and that's only a maybe. Dennis Weaver, Carol Channing, Ray Bradbury, Leslie Nielsen, Buzz Aldrin and many more came to Palm Springs at my request.

Lastly, a lifelong love of books and Palm Springs history has allowed me to inuitively know what earlier books would be useful while researching the material for this book. You'll find a list in the back.

So please read, converse and share the histories herein. And especially, email me your own stories.

Little Tuscany

Eric G. Meeks Colllection

LITTLE TUSCANY

Resting on the idyllic rocky outcroppings fronting Chino Canyon and the lofty spires of San Jacinto, this enclave of homes was originally developed in 1935 by local realtor Rufus Chapman and from its narrow curvy streets, reminiscent of its European namesake, one quickly spots glimpses of the city to the east and realizes that many of the homes are perched to maximize uniquely spectacular views.

The neighborhood winds from Highway 111 on the east to Tuscany Heights Drive in the West and from West Vista Chino on its southern border to Tramway Road on the North.

You may also be pleasantly surprised, as I was when driving its streets, at the variations in the homes here. Some have the quaintness of early settlers handmade structures, made from the scrubbed rocks of the hills themselves, humble in their craftsmanship, yet sturdy in their nature. Other homes are magnificent edifices of modernistic design, beyond belief in their grandeur; icons to the men and women who's personalities were as large as the screens they illuminated, the stages they played upon or the board rooms they directed from. Still others fall somewhere in between.

And yet, though each person had their moment or more in the sunny spotlight, not every player's scene, upon life's grand stage, ended happily.

Little Tuscany

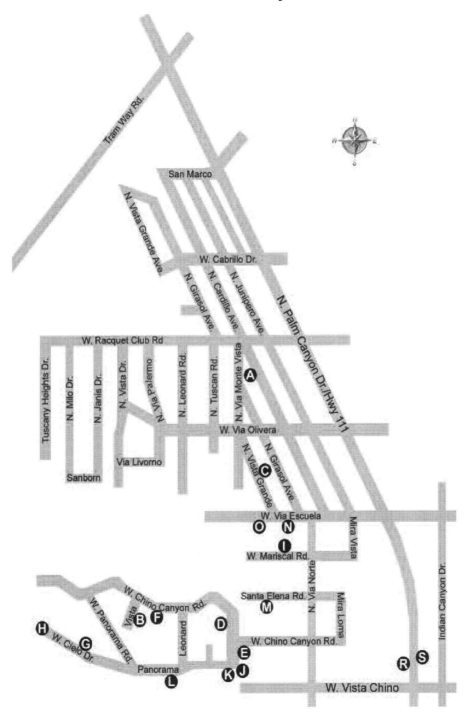

Ⓐ 2481 North Cardillo Road
TOM NEAL

This boxer turned actor moved here with his third wife Gail Evatt when there was no more denying his once leading man persona was over and gone. It was in this home that on April Fool's Day in 1965 Neal murdered his wife with a .45 pistol after demanding sex and ripping her clothes off her, while accusing his already divorce seeking wife of cheating.

His glory days of WWII stardom had begun fading 15 years before when he'd committed assault with his fists of fury on then girlfriend Barbara Paytons' lover, Franchot Tone. Neal slaughtered Tone. He won the fight but lost Barbara. She married Franchot.

It is believed that as his star fell and he was reduced first to being a Matre'D at the Doll House restaurant, where he took reservations of former colleagues, and eventually succumbed to landscaping work to pay the bills, his life became even more disconsolate. After taking one last stab at re-energizing his career with a script based on the gruesome Black Dahlia Murders, he gave up. The script was well received. Neal was not.

In an effort to reconcile with his creditors and Gail, he sold his Movie Colony estate and moved out to Cardillo Road, then considered the edge of town, where some say he diverted Black Dahlia investment money into this 3 bed 3 bath 1964 home before being sentenced to ten years in prison in Indio Superior Court on First Degree Murder. He died in 1972 at the age of 58.

Ⓑ 1860 North Vista Drive
WILLIAM EDRIS

Business tycoon and hotelier (Seattle's famed Olympic Hotel), WIlliam Edris owned this 1942 3 bed 3 bath 2,038sf home on a 16,117sf lot. It was one of two houses he owned in the Little Tuscany area of Palm Springs in 1954.

Ⓒ 2200 North Vista Grande
MARC LAWRENCE

Bad guy actor known for playing mobsters and killers commonly called Lefty owned this 1,711sf 3 bed 2 bath home on a 10,454sf lot from 1977 till 2006. He had a list of credits stretching more than 70 years. Some of his films include: *G Men* with James Cagney (1935), *Marathon Man* with Dustin Hoffman(1976), *The Dukes of Hazard* (1979), 4 different *Star Trek* episodes, and Schwazeneggers' *End of Days*(1999).

Ⓓ 623 West Chino Canyon Road
ERNST KRENEK

in 1965, the Austrian composer lived in this 3 bed 2 bath 2,005sf home with a pool on a 16,117sf lot. It was built in 1958.

He was born in Vienna and studied in Berlin before performing in German opera houses until his music was banned by the Nazi party for including renditions of American Negro Jazz.

He moved to the United States in 1938 where a decade later he married Gladys Nordenstrom, a student of his.

Ⓔ 595 West Chino Canyon Drive

ZSA ZSA GABOR

Zsa Zsa never owned this 4 bedroom 6 bath 6,101sf home, but she did live in it sometime between when it was contructed in 1968 and 1988, when it was bought by Jean and Hamilton Garland, a Los Angeles Fashion designer.

During these years, Zsa Zsa was married to three different men. One of them, inventor Jack Ryan, who designed the Barbie Doll and while their marriage was falling apart disassembled her Rolls Royce and refused to put it back together again.

All the Gabor ladies owned homes in Palm Springs throughout the 1950's to the late 1990's.

F 845 West Chino Canyon Road

THE JERGENS FAMILY

In 1946, the Jergens family, of bathroom products fame, hired Albert Frey to design this Spanish colonial 3 bed 4 bath home with 3,000sf of interior space, positioned upon a 76,230sf hill lot with a pool. The family then sold it to Elton F. McDonald, a supermarket whiz who stayed an owner for years before selling it to Elvis and Priscilla Presley for $105,000. Elvis put $20k down.

ELVIS PRESLEY

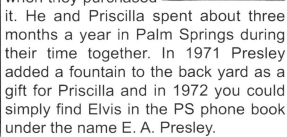

The King of Rock and Roll owned this home from 1970-1977. He bought it as a reminder to his honeymoon days in Palm Springs with his wife Priscilla. Lisa Marie was 2 years old when they purchased it. He and Priscilla spent about three months a year in Palm Springs during their time together. In 1971 Presley added a fountain to the back yard as a gift for Priscilla and in 1972 you could simply find Elvis in the PS phone book under the name E. A. Presley.

Elvis especially enjoyed the night time temperatures in the desert. Because of the warm evenings it was the

Elvis Presley continued...

perfect time to enjoy the outdoors and the pool while avoiding paparrazi and invading fans. He was known to menacingly throw water balloons at anyone coming to the front door he thought deserved a wet joke.

But after his divorce from Priscilla in 1973, the home took on more of a boy's club persona. During Elvis's solo ownership of the property he added a basketball hoop to the end of the driveway and placed a roof over the 16-person Jacuzzi to prevent photographers in helicopters from taking snap shots at him during the daytime. He also added an entertainment room (called the Jungle Room), two bath rooms, a personal bedroom suite and a sauna. It now has 5,040sf of interior space.

He was known to purchase Cadillac's at Plaza Motors. According to Andy Jessup, Jr., Elvis came in during the dead of summer. "A black Caddy had just come in from the factory. It was in the back. Elvis saw it. Wanted it. WAS gonna buy it.....until we couldn't find the keys!!" The same day, he went and bought a black Lincoln from Palm Springs Lincoln Mercury.

Elvis was also known to shoot out his televisions here. Ken Parker, owner of Hallmark TV downtown Palm Springs, was called upon twice to deliver big screen televisions to replace the shot out sets after Elvis saw Robert Goulet on them.

Elvis remodeled the living room with acoustical tiles and recorded nine songs here, including: Are you Sincere, Blue Spanish Eyes, I Miss You, and Sweet Angeline. Once, while recording here, Elvis busted his microphone stand and simply taped a mic to a mop in a bucket as an impromptu stand.

Elvis spent his last birthday here and after Elvis' death, Priscilla Presley sold it to American musician **Frankie Valli**.

In January of 2014, the home was put on the marlet for $3,950,000. Deemed to be a steal for what was condiered the second most valuable piece of Elvis memorabilia in existence. The first most significant would of course be Graceland in Memphis, Tennessee.

Ⓖ 1030 West Cielo Drive

WILLIAM EDRIS

Business tycoon and owner of the Seattle Olympic Hotel. He owned two Palm Springs homes simultaneously in 1954. This one was designed by E. William Stewart and was built in 1952 with a V-shaped roof, 2 bedrooms 3 baths and 2,700sf of space on a 26,136sf lot with a pool overlooking the valley.

Ⓘ 444 West Mariscal Road

ROD TAYLOR

Australian born Taylor started acting in Hollywood in 1951. He's starred in *The Time Machine* (1960), *The Birds* (1963), many TV shows, and his most recent role was as Winston Churchill in Quentin Tarantino's *Inglorious Basterds*.

In 1967 he bought this 4 bed 3 bath, 3,214sf home, built in 1965 on 20,038sf lot.

(H) 1090 West Cielo Drive

MAGDA GABOR

The oldest of the Gabor sisters lived in this 3,441sf home from when it was new in 1964 till her death in 1997. It has 4 bedrooms 4 baths, a pool, and sits on a 26,136sf lot.

Magda was married six times, four of them for roughly a year or less. Her fifth husband, George Sanders (Mr. Freeze from Batman fame) had been Zsa Zsa's third husband. They were married in Indio Courthouse and had a reception at the Racquet Club. Their union was annulled after only three months. In 1972 Sanders committed suicide.

The beautiful Gabor sisters - pictured below: Zsa Zsa, Magda, and Eva - were of Hungarian descent and each became actresses and socialites in America after fleeing Europe in WWII.

Magda died in Palm Springs of Kidney failure at the age of 82, only two months after the death of her mother, Jolie.

They are both buried in Desert Memorial Park in Cathedral City.

🅙 600 West Panorama Road

RAYMOND LOEWY

Loewy was the industrial designer credited with the modern Coca-Cola bottle, the Greyhound bus, Schick Razors and more. This home was designed by Albert Frey and built in 1944. It has 2,066sf, 5 bedrooms 4 bathrooms, a pool and sits on a 39,204sf lot.

K 701 West Panorama Road
GEORGE RANDOLPH
& ROSALIE HEARST

The son of William Randolph Hearst owned this 7 bed 6 bath 7,557sf home, built in 1962 on a 27,007sf lot with a pool. It's claimed that Patricia Hearst recuperated here after her trial for bank robbing in the 1970's. Rosalie was a long-time Palm Springs philanthropist known for helping found the Palm Springs Womens Press Club and many other charitable organizations.

L 815 West Panorama Road
FREDERICK LOEWE

Austrian born composer whose credits include'*Brigadoon(1954)*, *My Fair Lady('64)*, *Camelot('67)* and *Paint Your Wagon('69)*, purchased this 4,369sf 1956 home in 1960. It has 4 bedrooms and 5 baths, a 3 hole chipping and putting golf course, a tennis court and a pool on a well manicured 42,253sf lot.

Ⓜ 485 West Santa Elena Road

DENNIS DAY

Child sidekick to Jack Benny and one of the original Mouseketeers from the Mickey Mouse Club owned this 2,902sf 3 bed 3 bath 1953 home on a 18,731sf lot.

Ⓝ 447 Via Escuela

DON CASTLE

Actor with close resemblance to Clark Gable, who played multiple roles, including: *Gun Fight at the OK Corral*, but never really caught on owned this 5 bed 5 bath home. It was built in 1948 and has 3,781sf on a 20,038sf lot. He was also Associate Producer on 63 episodes of *Lassie*.

◎ 483 West Via Escuela
TRISTAN ROGERS

Actor who has played Doctor Robert Scipio on *General Hospital* for 11 seasons currently owns this 4 bed 4 bath 1948 home, with 3,472sf on a 20,038sf lot. He bought it in 1997. He's been acting since 1967.

® 1777 North Palm Canyon Drive
LA FONTAINE RETREAT

Former home of murderous criminal Sante Kimes who went on a 30 year spree of killing and cons: 1968-1998. She was eventually caught and convicted of killing New York socialite Irene Silverman. Her crimes included: arson, burglary, fraud, enslavement and three murders.

Ⓢ 1800 North Palm Canyon Drive
BILLY REED'S RESTAURANT

Named for Vaudeville entertainer and New York operator of the clubs: Copacabana, El Morocco, and the Little Club, Billy Reeds opened in 1974, the same year the entertainer died.

MARION DAVIES'

The Desert Inn

"Palm Springs' Distinguished Hotel"

Continental Breakfast
Bungalow Type Accommodations
20-Acre Garden Estate in the Center of Village

OLYMPIC-SIZED POOL
PRIVATE HEALTH CLUB
for Men and Women
ROCK STEAM BATHS - MASSAGE

FAirview 4-1171

153 N. PALM CANYON DR.   PALM SPRINGS

from the 1958 Palm Springs Phone Directory.

Palm Springs Historical Society

Ann Miller playing around at The Racquet Club circa 1940.

RACQUET CLUB

A neighborhood which grew up around a hotel that made a name for itself by attracting more stars than it could house. This would become a familiar theme in Palm Springs that would be recreated in both the Movie Colony and the downtown core.

It's been claimed that the original Racquet Club was built after actors Charlie Farrell and Ralph Bellamy were kicked off the El Mirador Hotels tennis courts for not being paid guests. Shortly thereafter, while horse back riding on the edge of town, they came upon a handpainted sign on a vacant windswept lot stating 55 acres for sale by PS Water Company owner and local devloper Alvah Hicks. $3500 later, Farrell and Bellamy held the deed.

The club was built in a haphazard way, as the needs to meet guests demands escalalted over only a few years. Tennis courts first, main structures second, rooms last. There was even a point when they charged for sodas, yet gave beer away for free. Because they had yet to get a liquor license.

The homes in the area grew in the same way as some of the guests sought more permanent residences close to the club.

At times I've wondered, 'What was the attraction to the desert of so many?'

To the best of my knowledge it came down to two main factors, besides the abundant sunshine, warmth and clean living environment which still prevail today. First, it was that, at the time, many of the studios had a 100 mile clause in the performers contracts limiting how far the actors and actresses could travel from the production lot. And secondly, the American media machine was alive and well, yet not so paparrazziesque to forbid the stars a private life. Many of them would even list their phone numbers openly in the PS phone directory. These elements mixed beautifully to create a very unique playground to the stars.

Racquet Club

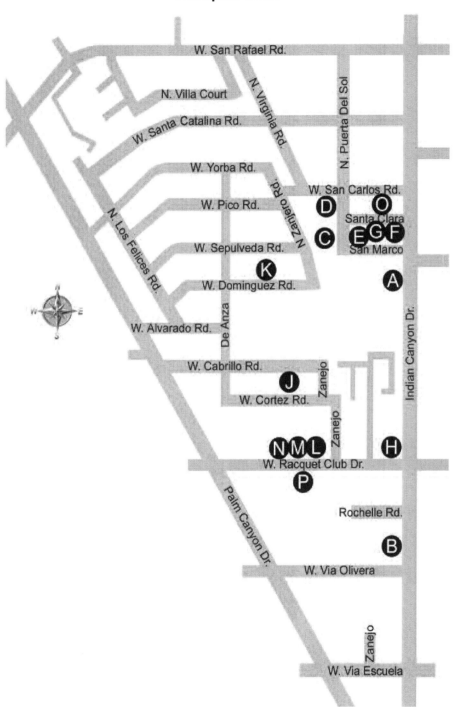

Ⓐ 2743 North Indian Canyon Drive
THE RACQUET CLUB

This historic club opened its doors on December 15, 1934 and was owned by actors Charlie Farrell (Mr. Palm Springs) and Ralph Bellamy.

In its hey day, the 175 one and two bedroom villas housed the Hollywood elite, including Clark Gable, Spencer Tracy, Joan Crawford, Marilyn Monroe, Lucy and Desi Arnaz and many, many more.

Unfortunately, as the 1970's and later decades passed, the resort fell into a period of lackluster repurchases and failed revitalizations. Its villas were too spread out, too far at the edge of town and too unprofitable in it's old time construction and now, when you drive past, it's but a demolition site with few buildings remaining, barely a shadow of its former glory.

Ⓑ 2311 North Indian Canyon Drive
GRACE LEWIS MILLER

Home designed by Richard Neutra and built in 1937 for the socialite, actress, fitness instructor and authoress. It has 3 bedrooms 3 baths, 1,398sf of interior space and sits on a 21,780sf lot. Lewis also wrote a screenplay about explorers Merriwether Lewis and William Clark, which went unproduced, but she did become a leading authority on the duo.

CHARLIE FARRELL

Actor and owner of The Racquet Club, Charlie Farrell, also at one time owned this home.

Here Farrell is shown with guest, Marilyn Monroe.

Farrell lived to be nearly 90 years old. After his death, apparently there were some discrepancies in his claimed age.

He is laid to rest in the Welwood Murray Cemetery in the Las Palmas neighborhood.

Ⓒ 2905 North Puerta Del Sol

CHARLES BUTTERWORTH

Journalist and baritoned actor who spoke the famous line "Why don't you get out of those wet clothes and get into a dry martini?" owned this home till he died in 1946.

ROBERT HORNSTEIN

Heir to Puss 'n' Boots cat food fortune lived in this 7 bedroom 7 bath estate in 1951. It's called "The Sunset" and was built in 1935 with 4,743sf on a 41,382sf lot. It is claimed that Joan Crawford was his house guest here in 1953.

JANE WYMAN

Actress leased this home from Hornstein after the miscarriage of her third child and subsequent divorce from Ronald Reagan in 1951.

That same year, Wyman received her third Oscar nomination for her role in *The Blue Veil*.

From 1981 to 1990, she starred in the night time CBS soap opera, *Falcon Crest*, as the tyrannical matriarch Angela Channing.

Ⓓ 2965 North Puerta Del Sol

PAUL LUKAS

Leading man actor built this 3,335sf home in 1935 for $4,750. It has 3 bedrooms 4 baths, a pool, and sits on a 37,462sf lot.

Lukas made 47 films from 1922 to 1970. In 1933, he played Athos in *The Three Musketeers* and in 1943 he won the Best Actor award for his portrayal of a man working against the Nazi's in *Watch on the Rhine* opposite Betty Davis.

Ⓔ 166 West San Marcos Way

MERVYN LEROY

The Producer of *Wizard of Oz* and Director of *Little Caesar, No Time For Sargeants* and *Gypsy* bought this 3 bed 3 bath 2,914sf 1956 home to reminisce about his 1946 honeymoon at the Racquet Club. He started his Hollywood career in the costume dept.

F 153 West Santa Clara Way

ARMAND DEUTSCH

Grandson of Julius Rosenwald, founder of Sears, Roebuck and Company, Deutsch became a movie producer with MGM and Warner Brothers. He bought this home new in 1948. It was built in 1947 with 4 bedrooms 3 baths, 2,646sf on a 16,117sf lot with a pool. Here he is shown with his wife Harriet.

G 165 West Santa Clara Way

ALEXANDER HALL

Director of *Little Miss Marker* and *My Sister Eileen*, owned this 5 bed 4 bath 3,326sf home in 1952. It sits on an 11,761sf lot with a pool.

JACK LAMBERT

Character actor Lambert married Alexander Hall's divorcee wife, Marjorie Franklin and moved into this home in 1959.

Ⓗ The Racquet Club Colony

MORGANA KING

Jazz Singer of the disco hit "A Taste of Honey," who also played Marlon Brando's wife in *Godfather I and II*, lived in these condos in 1999. They were designed by William F. Cody and built by George and Robert Alexander.

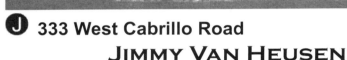

Ⓙ 333 West Cabrillo Road

JIMMY VAN HEUSEN

Songwriter, whose real name was Chester Edward Babcock, lived here from 1948-1951. The home was built in 1937 with 3 bedrooms 2 baths, 1,433sf on a 7,841sf lot. In 1951, when Frank Sinatra had marital troubles with Ava Gardner, he took up residence here with his friend Van Heusen.

Ⓚ 352 West Dominguez Road
COLLEEN APPLEGATE (SHAUNA GRANT)

X-rated actress committed suicide with a pistol to the head in this 3 bed 2 bath 1,225sf home on March 21, 1984 owned by her boyfriend, downtown PS business owner Jake Ehrlich. (Pelle's Leather Goods)

Ⓛ 215 West Racquet Club Road
MILTON BREN

Bren negotiated the sale of *The Wizard of Oz* to MGM and used this home in 1939-40.

Ⓜ 251 West Racquet Club Road
EDWARD SMALL

Independent Producer lived here in 1938.

Ⓝ 283 West Racquet Club Road
FRANK SHIELDS

Tennis Champ who played bit parts and is Brooke Shields Granddad lived here in 1938.

All three of these homes have been replaced by condos.

⊙ 133 West San Carlos Road

SAMUEL BRISKIN

Co-Founder of Liberty Films, producer of *It's a Wonderful Life*, owned this 3 bed, 3 bath, 1,720sf home built in 1947 on a 7,841sf lot.

℗ 287 West Racquet Club Road

GRETA GARBO

Unverified story of Garbo recuperating here after breaking up with *Flesh and the Devil* co-star John Gilbert in 1926 when she supposedly jilted him at the altar. It is thought she fled when her romance was discovered by her mentor and former lover, Jack Stiller.

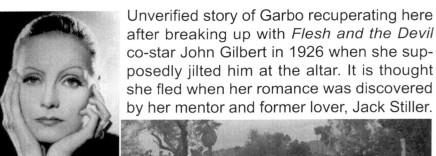

Eric G. Meeks Colllection

Bob Hope in the buffet line at The Racquet Club in the 1950's.

Palm Springs Historical Society

Clark Gable and Charlie Farrell playing a game of lawn chess at The Racquet Club in the 1950's.

RACQUET CLUB ESTATES

These family-sized residences sprouted as the city reached from its celebrity sproutings and reached for a burgeoning upper middle-class in the 1950's and 60's.

A father(George) and son(Bob) building team, who would become legendary in their own right, would create a legacy of simple post, beam and glass constructed homes that would attract the growing affluent class of Los Angeles semi-elite to invest in a permanent vacation destination or cast their die of chance and partake of the desert's blossoming opportunities.

If I could cast a categorical reference on the matter - which of course, I can - I'd say that the Racquet Club Estates shine brightly in the Silver Age of Palm Springs. The Golden Age being the El Mirador and Racquet Club Hotel eras. The new home owners were comprised of second and third generation Hollywood elite. Some were affluent men and women seeking a bit of the legendary sunshine and effervescent atmosphere which is Palm Springs. All of them wanted a piece of paradise Together, these celebrities and business people came to bear fruit within the budding palm tree lined, though still single-laned, streets of the Village of Palm Springs.

While there is the occasional pioneer's home of older heritage, the vast majority of these properties were built after 1958 and more appropriately ends at Avenida Caballerors on the east. But for the sake of this book, this chapter shall encompass all the way from Indian Canyon Drive on the west to Sunrise Way on the east and from San Rafael on the north to Vista Chino on the south.

Racquet Club Estates

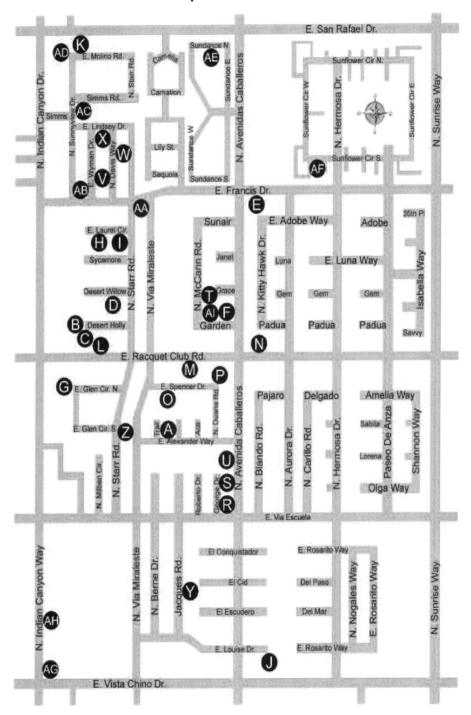

Ⓐ 666 Alexander Way

HY AVERBACK

Actor-director moved into this 3 bed 2 bath home in 1968. It was built in 1959, has 1,225sf and sits on a 11,326sf lot with a pool. During WWII, he created a comical character Tokyo Mose, lampooning the Japanese's Tokyo Rose.

Ⓑ 309 East Desert Holly Circle

ALAN FREED

In 1964, the Disc Jockey, aka Moondog, who first coined the phrase "Rock and Roll" while offering a mix of blues, country and rhythm and blues, lived in this 3 bed 2 bath, 1,225sf home, built in 1959 on a 11,326sf lot. Unfortunately for Freed, his career was ruined by the 'Payola' scandal that hit the music industry in the early 1960's. Freed died in PS on Jan. 20, 1965.

© 315 East Desert Holly Circle

RUTA LEE

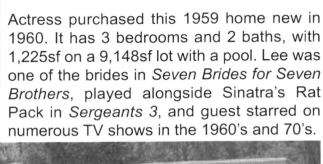

Actress purchased this 1959 home new in 1960. It has 3 bedrooms and 2 baths, with 1,225sf on a 9,148sf lot with a pool. Lee was one of the brides in *Seven Brides for Seven Brothers*, played alongside Sinatra's Rat Pack in *Sergeants 3*, and guest starred on numerous TV shows in the 1960's and 70's.

ⓓ 511 East Desert Willow Drive

DARREN MCGAVIN

Actor, best known for playing the title role in the television horror series *Kolchak: The Night Stalker* and as the father in the holiday classic *A Christmas Story*, purchased this 1959 Alexander home in 1960. It has 1,225sf 3 bed 2 bath on a 10,454sf lot.

E 1033 East Francis Road
CHEETA

Star of multiple *Tarzan* movies and *Bedtime for Bonzo* with Ronald Reagan. The Cheeta Primate Sanctuary home has been owned by Cheeta's care giver Daniel Westfall since 1988. Besides the now gray haired Cheeta's private chambers the home is a 3 bed 2 bath 1,225sf Alexander, built in 1961 with a pool on a 10,454sf lot. Cheeta is known to enjoy his beer.

🅕 980 East Garden Road
BILLY DANIELS, JR.

Son of the Singer Billy Daniels Sr. lived in this 1,667sf, 4 bedroom 3 bathroom Alexander home built in 1961.

🅖 352 East Glen Circle North
ARTHUR E. ARLING

Oscar Winning Cameraman for Best Color Cinematography for *Gone With The Wind* and *The Yearling*, Arling bought this 3 bed 2 bath 1,225sf home in 1970. It was built in 1959 with a pool on a 14,810sf lot. Here he is shown with Betty Grable while on the set of *Wabash Avenue*.

H 407 East Laurel Circle

JOHN PAYNE

Actor, whose most famous role was that of attorney Fred Gailey in *Miracle on 34th Street*, retired to this 3 bed 2 bath 1,791sf home on a 10,454sf lot in 1961. Later in his career he switched to tough guy roles in Film Noir and westerns. In 1955 he paid a $1000 a month option for the rights to the James Bond book *Moonraker*, but gave it up when he discovered he could not retain the rights to all the bond novels.

I 581 East Laurel Circle

ALEX GOTTLIEB

Writer and Producer of dozens of movies including *Abbott & Costello Meet Captain Kidd*. Gottlieb and his wife, Polly Rose, lived in this 3 bed 2 bath home with 1,603sf of interior space on a 10,454sf lot with a pool.

Ⓙ 1165 East Louise Drive

HAL POLAIRE

Four decades in film production, including being Assistant Director on *Some Like it Hot* and Production Manager on *Rocky*, Polaire has lived here since 1994. The 1,460sf home was built in 1978 with 3 bedrooms 2 baths & a pool on a 10,019sf lot.

Ⓚ 330 East Molino Road

JIM ISERMANN

Los Angeles multiplicity artist purchased this 2 bed 3 bath 1,854sf 1962 home in 1997. It was designed by Donald Wexler.

Ⓛ 412 East Racquet Club Road

ALBERT SALMI

Actor who played villains lived in this 3 bed, 2 bath, 1,225sf home in 1965. It sits on an 11,326sf lot. In 1967 he recieved the Western Heritage Wrangler Award from the Cowboy Hall of Fame.

Ⓜ 757 East Racquet Club Road

DEBBIE REYNOLDS

Alexander home of the actress, which she owned from 1963-1987. It's a 3 bed 2 bath with 1,225sf on a 10,019sf lot with a pool. While living here Reynolds played Molly Brown in *The Unsinkable Molly Brown*(1962), had her own TV series *The Debbie Reynolds Show(1969-70)* and made appearances on *The Love Boat* three times.

N 1050 East Racquet Club Road

JACKIE COOGAN

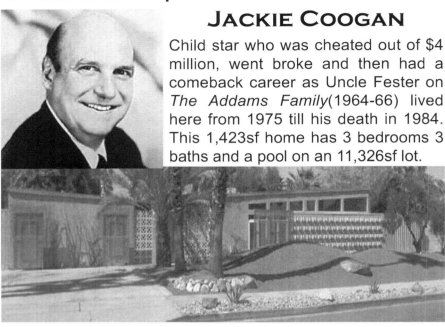

Child star who was cheated out of $4 million, went broke and then had a comeback career as Uncle Fester on *The Addams Family*(1964-66) lived here from 1975 till his death in 1984. This 1,423sf home has 3 bedrooms 3 baths and a pool on an 11,326sf lot.

O 715 East Spencer Drive

MR. BLACKWELL

Real name Richard Selzer, lived here with boyfriend/hairstylist Robert Spencer who built the 1,225sf 3 bed 2 bath home in 1959.

🅟 888 East Spencer Drive
HENRY LEVIN

Director of *Journey to the Center of the Earth*(1959), *Where the Boys Are*(1960) and three episodes of *Knott's Landing*(1980) and scores of other projects, Levin bought this home in 1961. It was built in 1959 with 1,333sf, 3 bedrooms 2 baths on an 11,326sf lot with a pool.

🅡 2108 George Drive
STUBBY KAYE

Began his career in 1939 by winning a radio contest. In his 50 years in film, Kaye appeared in *Guys and Dolls*, *The Alfred Hitchcock Hour, Adam-12, Laverne and Shirley,* and played Marvin Acme in *Who Framed Roger Rabbit*.

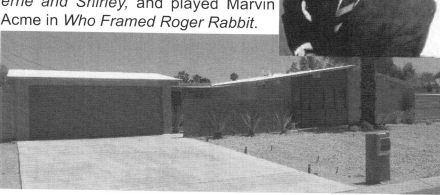

Ⓢ 2126 George Drive

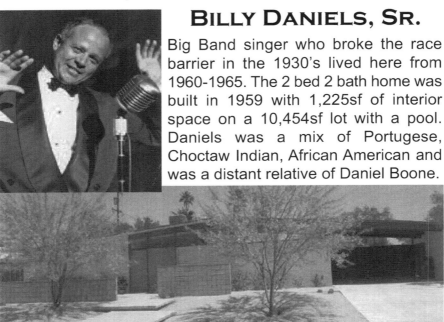

BILLY DANIELS, SR.

Big Band singer who broke the race barrier in the 1930's lived here from 1960-1965. The 2 bed 2 bath home was built in 1959 with 1,225sf of interior space on a 10,454sf lot with a pool. Daniels was a mix of Portugese, Choctaw Indian, African American and was a distant relative of Daniel Boone.

Ⓣ 811 Grace Circle

STEVE McQUEEN

Actor bought this 3 bed 3 bath 1,445sf 1961 home new where he took peyote bought from Indians in the high desert. He purchased this home with money from his roles in *The Blob*(1958), *The Magnificent Seven*(1960), and then made *The Great Escape*(1963).

(U) 2217 North Avenida Caballeros

PAUL BURKE

Actor who portrayed cops and cowboys bought this home new. It's a 1959 Alexander home with 3 bed, 2 bath in 2,400sf of interior space on a 10,019sf lot. His most famous role was as Lyon Burke in *Valley of the Dolls* (1967).

(V) 2839 North Davis Way

MILBURN STONE

Character actor who was in more than 150 pictures, but was most famously known for his portrayal of "Doc" Adams on *Gunsmoke*, which ran for 20 years on television from 1955-75, lived here with his wife, Jane Garrison, in 1959 when the 3 bed 2 bath 1,225sf home was new. It has a pool on a 10,019sf lot.

Ⓦ 2918 North Davis Way

RUSSELL ARMS

Actor who began his career in *The Man Who Came to Dinner* lived here from 1989-2004. The 1,463sf home was built in 1959 with 3 bedrooms 2 baths on a 10,019sf lot. His career was stalled by WWII and upon his return was on *Your Hit Parade*, a forerunner to *American Bandstand*.

Ⓧ 2981 North Davis Way

JACKIE COOPER

Child actor from the *Our Gang* comedies who made the transition into adult roles, such as playing News Editor Perry White in the *Superman* movies alongside Christopher Reeves. Cooper bought this 3 bed 2 bath home new in 1960. It has 1,632sf on a 10,019sf lot. Cooper was also a Captain in the Navy.

ⓨ 1866 North Jacques Drive

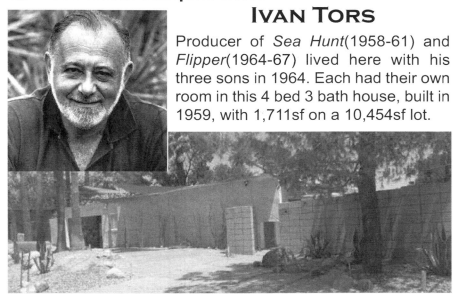

IVAN TORS

Producer of *Sea Hunt*(1958-61) and *Flipper*(1964-67) lived here with his three sons in 1964. Each had their own room in this 4 bed 3 bath house, built in 1959, with 1,711sf on a 10,454sf lot.

ⓩ 2294 North Starr Road

LEO TOVER

Cinematographer of *The Great Gatsby, The Day the Earth Stood Still, Journey to the Center of the Earth* and 110 other films lived in this 1,200sf 3 bed 2 bath home till he died in 1964. It was built in 1959 on a 10,890sf lot.

CLIFFORD STINE

1950's Science Fiction and Horror Cinematographer bought this home in 1965.

AA 2788 North Starr Road

PHIL FELDMAN

Producer of *The Wild Bunch*(1969) with Palm Springs long time resident William Holden, and *The Toy*(1982) with Richard Pryor lived owned this 1958 home in 1968. It has 3 bedrooms 2 baths with 1,188sf on a 10,454sf lot.

AB 2808 North Sunny View Drive

SY DEVORE

Tailor to the Stars built this 3 bed 2 bath home in 1959. It has 1,225sf & a pool on a 10,019sf lot. Devore was known to make suits for The Rat Pack, Elvis's Las Vegas outfits, Liberace's performance costumes and band uniforms for Tommy Dorsey. His list of clients was a who's who of Hollywood for 40 years.

(AC) 3100 North Sunny View Drive

STANLEY KRAMER

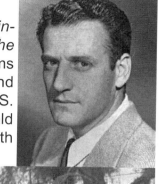

Producer of *Guess Who's Coming to Dinner*(1967), *The Caine Mutiny*(1954), *The Wild One*(1953), *High Noon*(1952), 40 films in all, owned this home at one time and lived in it with his wife and three kids. U.S. Steel House designed by architect Donald Wexler. Built in 1961. This is a 3 bed 2 bath home with 1,536sf on a 10,890sf lot.

JIM MOORE

GQ magazine Creative Director in charge of the fashion pages, creating the GQ look, bought this home in 1993. He is the recipient of fashions equivalent of a lifetime achievement award.

(AD) 3165 North Sunny View Drive

DOUGLAS KEEVE

Director bought this home in 1985. It was designed by Donald Wexler and built in 1962 with 2 bedrooms 2 baths, 1,477sf and a pool.

AE 2926 Sundance Circle West

CHERYL CRANE

Owned by the daughter of Lana Turner; who, at 14, was acquitted of stabbing Turner's abusive Mobster boyfriend Johnny Stompanato to death. At one time, in a fit of jealousy, Stompanato pointed a gun at Sean Connery. In 1996, Crane bought this 2 bed 2 bath 1,855sf condo, built in 1982.

AF 2807 Sunflower Loop South

VIVIAN AUSTIN

In 1996, actress who was voted Miss Hollywood in 1943 lived in this 2 bed 2 bath 1,068sf condo, built in 1984. Austin acted in 26 films during the 1930's and 1940's. She was also a stunt double and a leg model.

AG 1600 North Indian Canyon Drive

RIVIERA RESORT

Designed after its Las Vegas counterpart by Pacific Palisades architect Homer Rissman and built by Irwin Schuman in 1959 and at cost of $3 million. It is a colossal epicenter of mid-century modern design. Schuman also owned the Chi Chi Club in downtown Palm Springs, which hosted and starred many celebrities.

Eric G. Meeks Colllection
Construction of the Riviera Resort under way in 1963.

AH 1700 North Indian Canyon Drive

BONO'S RESTAURANT

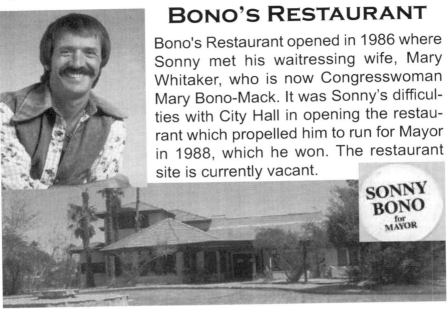

Bono's Restaurant opened in 1986 where Sonny met his waitressing wife, Mary Whitaker, who is now Congresswoman Mary Bono-Mack. It was Sonny's difficulties with City Hall in opening the restaurant which propelled him to run for Mayor in 1988, which he won. The restaurant site is currently vacant.

SONNY BONO for MAYOR

AI 914 East Garden Road

BILLY VAUGHN

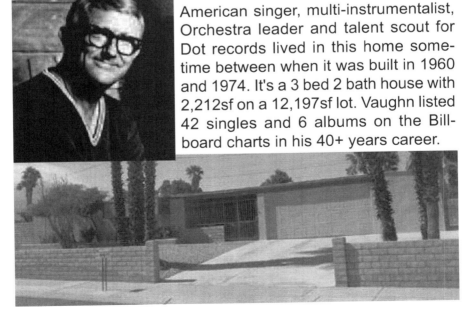

American singer, multi-instrumentalist, Orchestra leader and talent scout for Dot records lived in this home sometime between when it was built in 1960 and 1974. It's a 3 bed 2 bath house with 2,212sf on a 12,197sf lot. Vaughn listed 42 singles and 6 albums on the Billboard charts in his 40+ years career.

Paul Pospesil Colllection

Dean Martin, who was Frank Sinatra's #1 Rat Pack partner
and a remarkable crooner in his own right, enjoying a martini
at the Chi Chi Club downtown Palm Springs in the 1960's.

Palm Springs Historical Society

Spencer Tracy at The Racquet Club in the 1950's.

DESERT PARK ESTATES

While technically, Desert Park Estates covers only the homes from Sunrise to Farrell and Racquet Club to Vista Chino. This book will enlarge the neighborhood to cover the entire northern central section of homes all the way out to the Four Seasons neighborhood in the north and to Gene Autry Trail in the east.

This area of Palm Springs was literally nothing but shifting sand dunes till the first homes were built in the early 1950's. It's a large section of various builders and developers who have taken on mostly individual homes or small tracts. For these reasons you'll discover a variety of building styles, sizes and levels of luxury.

Considered more on the windy edge of town and in the flight path of the departing airplanes from the northern end of the runway, it is often overlooked by those seeking a more blue blood stature instead of blue collar. But for those who invest their hard earned dollars in this select area of Palm Springs they'll soon discover, much as a few celebrities did, that owners here enjoy unparalleled access to the more distant parts of the desert. Driveways are filled not with just the work trucks of middle America, but ATV's & motorcycles for some great desert romping fun and perhaps even nice boats and RV's for a more lengthy desert adventure that could allow stretches all the way out to the Colorado River and Glamis Dunes only 2 hours away.

Some of my best friends have lived in this part of town. It's where real people live real lives. Many of them provide the services necessary to get our food, our groceries, our appliances working, and more.

63

Desert Park Estates

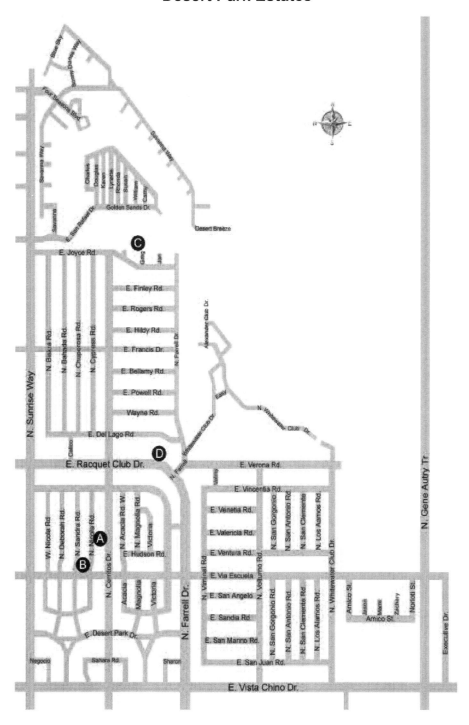

Ⓐ 2153 North Cerritos Road

SID TOMACK

Supporting actor who played waiters, con artists and other assorted bad guys in many films and especially on TV's *The Adventures of Superman*('52-58) opposite George Reeves and on *Perry Mason*('57-66) opposite Raymond Burr. Tomack lived in this 3 bed 2 bath 1,964sf 1960 home on an 11,761sf lot.

Ⓑ 2110 North Deborah Road

DON BARCLAY

In 1970, this Character actor of more than 80 films, including *Our Gang*(1922-44), *Frankenstein Meets the Wolf Man*(1943) and *Mary Poppins*(1964), retired to this 3 bed 2 bath 1,620sf 1958 home on a 11,761sf lot.

© 3099 North Greg Circle

SERGIO GALINDO

Mexican author of The Precipice(1960) and Otilia Rauda(1986), filmed as *La Mujer del Pueblo* in 2001 lived here from 1989-1993. The 1,608sf 4 bed 2 bath home was built in 1971.

Ⓓ 2388 East Racquet Club Road

TERRA COTTA INN

Formerly the Monkey Tree Inn during the time of it's claim to fame. Tom Mulhall, owner and operator of this clothing optional boutique resort says famed modernist architect Albert Frey told him room #34, with a private entrance, is where President John F. Kennedy and Marilyn Monroe had their fling. I find this hard to believe since Marilyn biographer Donald Spoto's research on the matter puts the tryst as happening in Bing Crosby's Palm Springs home. But it is possible the famous philandering couple met more than once and in more than one location; most would.

Palm Springs Historical Society

On the tarmac: Then President John F. Kennedy shaking hands with Mayor Frank Bogert after landing at Palm Springs International Airport circa 1962.

Las Palmas

Eric G. Meeks Colllection

An aerial photo of the Las Palmas neighborhood in the 1950's.

LAS PALMAS

The A-List of celebrity homes begins with this prestigious neighborhood nestled under the high rocky cliffs of Dry Falls Canyon. Before the first of these homes were built in the 1920's only big horn sheep and Cahuilla indians lived here. But today, these incrediblly beautiful, large, and often walled, estates are the best location to view the homes of top celebrities and the dwellings of Palm Springs most affluent pioneers.

Originally subdivided by Palm Springs Water President and realtor Alvah Hicks, he and his son, Harold, built the first twenty homes here, and the Church of Our Lady of Solitude on West Alejo Road.

The celebrities flocked to this neighborhood like migrating geese to water. The large lots inspired many of them to build unique desert edifices to glorify their personalities as they shifted from El Mirador, Racquet Club and small hotel guests into permanent primary and second home residents.

These are the homes of first generation settlers and celebrities. You'll find the names of many of the stars of the Golden Age of the Silver Screen, the movers and shakers of Hollywood royalty, and the barons of American business.

Many of them hired the best and brightest of Architects, engineers and contractors to build their Lost Horizon paradise under the welcome shadow of San Jacinto and within a stones throw of the restaurants, night clubs, retailers, and horse rentals, which provided the daily and nightly activities of Palm Springs.

Take your time and drive slow, the Las Palmas neighborhood will not disappoint your star gazing desires. It never has.

69

Las Palmas

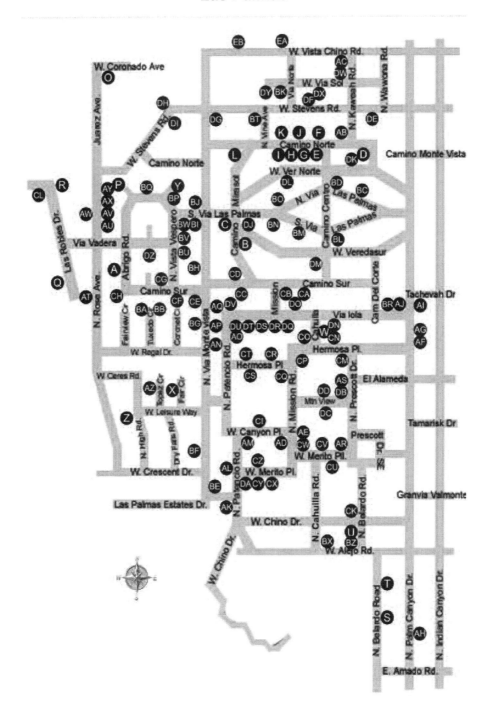

Ⓐ 1139 Abrigo Road
TRINI LOPEZ, JR.

Actor-Singer has owned this 4 bed 4 bath 2,521sf 1961 home on a 12,197sf lot since 1981. Lopez made thirty albums in his career with more than twenty top songs. He also co-starred in movies, including the 1967 hit *The Dirty Dozen*.

Ⓑ 1184 Camino MIrasol North
DONNA REED

Actress owned this home until her divorce in 1971. It was built in 1934 with 7 bedrooms 6 baths on a 31,799sf lot. Reed acted in more than 50 shows from 1941-85 including her own TV show *The Donna Reed Show*(1958-66), *It's a Wonderful Life* (1946) and won a Best Actress Oscar for her role in *From Here to Eternity*(1953) playing opposite Frank Sinatra.

© 1255 Camino Mirasol North

BUDDY ADLER

20th Century Fox Head of Production and a founding member of the Screen Actors Guild lived here with his actress wife Anita Louise until Adler's death in 1960. The 3 Bed 5 bath 3,003sf home, 15,026sf lot, was built in 1951.

CLAUDETTE COLBERT

Oscar winning actress for *It Happened One Night* with Clark Gable lived here in 1958.

Ⓓ 201 Camino Norte West

IRWIN SCHUMAN

Chi-Chi Club founder and resort builder, including the Riviera Resort lived in this 4 bedroom 6 bath 4,540sf home.

NAT "KING" COLE

Singer stayed here between appearances at the Chi Chi Club in 1958. Cole, a smoker of three packs of Kool cigarettes a day died of lung cancer in February 1965.

E ## 317 Camino Norte West
DINAH SHORE &
GEORGE MONTGOMERY

Singing actress and cowboy actor couple built this 1954 home with 4 bedrooms and 5 baths, 3,308sf and a pool on a 14,810sf lot.

HAROLD MIRISCH

Youngest of Mirisch Brothers production team who made *Some Like It Hot*(1959) *The Magnificent Seven*(1960), *West Side Story*(1961), *The Great Escape*(1963), *The Pink Panther*(1963), *The Thomas Crowne Affaire*(1968), *In The Heat Of The Night*(1967) and many others, lived here till his death in 1968.

F ## 322 Camino Norte West
PAUL WHITEMAN

Orchestra bandleader of one of the most popular dance bands in the 1920's lived in this 3 bed 3 bath 1936 home with 2,018sf while working at Romanoff's On The Rocks in 1964.

Ⓖ 323 Camino Norte West

ALAN LADD

Suicide or accidental death? Ladd over-dosed on barbituates and alcohol here in 1964. This 5 bed 5 bath 3,667sf 1955 home was designed by Donald Wexler and built on a 15,682sf lot. A year earlier, the *Shane* star, claimed to have accidentally shot himself in the chest at his Camarillo home.

Ⓗ 335 Camino Norte West

HOWARD HUGHES

America's first billionaire who ran profitable enterprises with everything from aeronau-tics to movies while dating starlets until he eventually became an overly compulsive germaphobe and shut out the world lived here. The 8,075sf home was built in 1940, 7 bdrm 10 bath on a 31,799sf double lot.

I 365 Camino Norte West
MARY MARTIN

Actress known for playing *Peter Pan*, *Sound of Music* and *South Pacific* lived in this 6 bedroom 5 bath 3,456sf home. It was built in 1936 on a 29,621sf lot with a pool, while Martin was married to her second husband, producer Richard Halliday. She is also the mother of actor Larry Hagman and was pregnant with him at 17 when she married her first husband.

J 372 Camino Norte West
ELVIS PRESLEY

Before the King of Rock and Roll rented his Hooneymoon Hideaway and long before he purchased Graceland West on Chino Canyon Road, Elvis rented this 3 bed 4 bath 3,348sf 1947 house with a pool on a 14,375sf lot.

Ⓚ 454 Camino Norte West

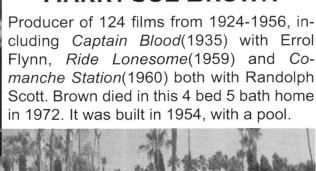

HARRY JOE BROWN

Producer of 124 films from 1924-1956, including *Captain Blood*(1935) with Errol Flynn, *Ride Lonesome*(1959) and *Comanche Station*(1960) both with Randolph Scott. Brown died in this 4 bed 5 bath home in 1972. It was built in 1954, with a pool.

Ⓛ 533 Camino Norte West

JOSEPH BARBERA

Co-creator of *Tom & Jerry, The Flintstones, Yogi Bear, Scooby-Doo* and other Hannah-Barbera cartoons owned this large 3 bed 5 bath 4,360sf home for at least 21 years, 1980-2001; the year he died. Built in 1938 on a 39,640sf lot, the Barbera Trust owns it.

Ⓞ ## 925 Coronado Avenue

LOUIS TAUBMAN

Oklahoma Oilman is the longtime owner of this 9,620sf 5 bed 10 bath home on a 66,211sf lot. It was visited by Lyndon Johnson in 1964, when brand new. Later, it hosted a dinner party for the Sinatra's, the Douglas's, Alan Hamel and Suzanne Somers.

Ⓟ ## 1350 Ladera Circle

ROBERT ALEXANDER
HOUSE OF TOMORROW

William Krisel designed and built by Robert Alexander in 1960 for his wife Helene. This 5 bed 5 bath 4,695sf home on a 15,246sf lot is a showpiece of the PS modern designed houses.

ELVIS & PRISCILLA

The famous Honeymoon Hideaway of the King and his bride, who intended to marry in PS, yet escaped the reporters camped out front and flew to Vegas in Sinatra's borrowed plane to be wed on May, 1, 1967.

ⓠ 1155 Los Robles Drive
CINDY WILLIAMS

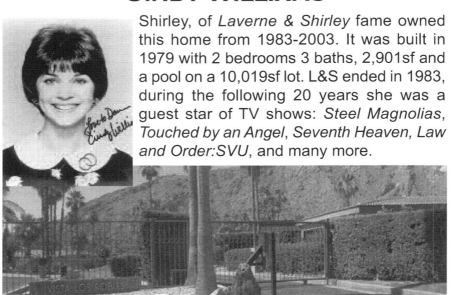

Shirley, of *Laverne & Shirley* fame owned this home from 1983-2003. It was built in 1979 with 2 bedrooms 3 baths, 2,901sf and a pool on a 10,019sf lot. L&S ended in 1983, during the following 20 years she was a guest star of TV shows: *Steel Magnolias*, *Touched by an Angel*, *Seventh Heaven*, *Law and Order:SVU*, and many more.

ⓡ 1354 Los Robles Drive
LEW SHERRELL

Agent, who landed Adam West the role as *Batman* in 1960's, owned this 1,977sf 3 bed 2 bath home, built in 1963 on a 12,632sf lot, until his death in 1996. Sherrell has a star on the Palm Springs Walk of Stars on Palm Canyon Drive.

Ⓢ **400 North Belardo Road**

PEGGY RYAN DANCE STUDIO

The female lead in *Here Comes the Co-Eds*(1945) with Abbott and Costello, plus multiple musical comedies in the 1940's and 50's, and who later played Jenny on *Hawaii Five-O*(1968-1976) owned a dance studio here. Now it's The American Legion Hall.

Ⓣ **456 North Belardo Road**

DOROTHY MANNERS

Syndicated newspaper gossip columnist for the Hearst Corporation lived here in 1955. She spent her first 30 years in the news business as assistant to Louella Parsons. At 95, she died in her Palm Springs home in August, 1998.

Ⓤ 535 North Belardo Road

JEAN HARLOW

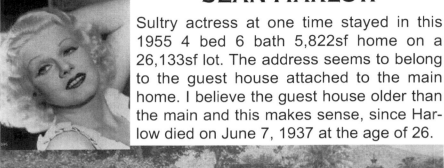

Sultry actress at one time stayed in this 1955 4 bed 6 bath 5,822sf home on a 26,133sf lot. The address seems to belong to the guest house attached to the main home. I believe the guest house older than the main and this makes sense, since Harlow died on June 7, 1937 at the age of 26.

Ⓦ 1050 North Cahuilla Road

STEPHEN SHAGAN

Novelist of nine best sellers, three of which were made into movies: *Save the Tiger*(1972), *City of Angels*(1975) and *The Formula*(1979) owned here with wife Elizabeth from 1990-2004. The 4 bed 3 bath 1934 home has 4,004sf on a 30,928sf lot.

CY HOWARD & BARBARA WARNER

Comedy Writer married to daughter of Jack L Warner (Warner Brothers) currently own this home

Ⓧ 845 North Fair Circle
BOBBY DARIN & SANDRA DEE

Singer of such hits as Dreamlover, Splish Splash and Mack The Knife was married to actress Sandra Dee while living in this 3 bed 2 bath 1,600sf home in 1964. It was built in 1960 on a 10,019sf lot. They were married from 1960-1967.

Ⓨ 1320 North Granito Circle
WILLIAM "BILL" MILLER

Entertainment Director of The Sahara in Las Vegas retired to this 3 bed 3 bath home in 1976. It has 3,249sf on a 14,810sf lot and was built in 1959.

Ⓩ 803 North High Road
JERRY HULSE

Los Angeles Times Travel Editor from 1960-1991 owned this home till his estate was settled in 1995. Built in 1961, the 3 bed 2 bath home was with 1,82sf, and a pool on a 10,890sf lot.

ⒶⒷ 1441 North Kaweah Road
WLADZIU VALENTINO LIBERACE

Famed pianist's third house in Palm Springs. It has a piano shaped black mailbox, 3 bedrooms 6 baths, 3,101sf, a 14,375 lot and was built in 1952. During his show business career Liberace went by several names: Walter Busterkeys, Walter Liberace, Lee Liberace, The Glitter Man and Mr. Showmanship. He owned a total of four homes in Palm Springs.

AC 1597 North Kaweah Road

H. BRUCE HUMBERSTONE

20th Century Fox Director of *Charlie Chan* and *Tarzan* movies, later he directed *The Smothers Brothers* and *Daniel Boone* TV shows, rented this 1,498sf 3 bed 3 bath 1951 home in 1957. Humberstone began his Hollywood career as a script clerk.

AD 775 North Mission Road

BUDDY RICH

Hailed as the World's Greatest Drummer, Rich lived in this 4 bed 5 bath 3.692sf home, built in 1952 on a 53,143sf lot. Rich played for such legendary bandleaders as Tommy Dorsey, Harry James & Les Brown.

AE 776 Morth Mission Road
SPENCER TRACY

Author Howard Johns, who wrote Palm Springs Confidential, claims it unlikely that Katherine Hepburn tended to an aging and ailing Spencer Tracy at this home, as some say, during the 1963 shooting of *It's a Mad Mad Mad Mad World* in the desert. Because Kirk Douglas says they were staying at his house.

AG 1050, 1060, 1068 North Palm Canyon Drive
SOL LESSER

Office building owned by Lesser who began his film career in 1915 at 25 with *The Last Night of the Barbary Coast*, depicting a crackdown of the whorehouses and gambling joints of San Francisco. Later, he produced the *Tarzan* films with Buster Crabbe, Johnny Weissmuller, and others.

AF ## 1032 North Palm Canyon Drive
THE DOLL HOUSE

At one time, The Doll House was a premier dinner house and nightclub, owned by George and Ethel Strebe, who also own the Plaza theatre. The house band was the Guadalajara Trio.

Legend has it that in 1953, Joan Crawford was dining here with Puss "n" Boots cat food corporation owner Robert Hornstein and after drinking too much Vodka went table to table pretending to be a waitress. Some people were thrilled, others delighted and a few refused to believe her act was a charade or that she was Joan Crawford.

Boxer turned actor Tom Neal was the maitre'd here when his career washed up and he was forced to seat many of the stars who were his former co-stars.

In the 1970's and 1980's it was Sorrentino's Restaurant. But today, it is just an empty lot.

AH 364 North Palm Canyon Drive
DOROTHY GRAY WOMEN'S CLOTHING

Owned by the fashion designer wife of Producer Harry Joe Brown. She only made 18 films from 1924-1948 and most of them in uncredited bit parts. Furthermore, she was no relation to the famous cosmetics queen Dorothy Gray, yet similarly named.

AI 1078 North Palm Canyon Drive
HOAGY CARMICHAEL

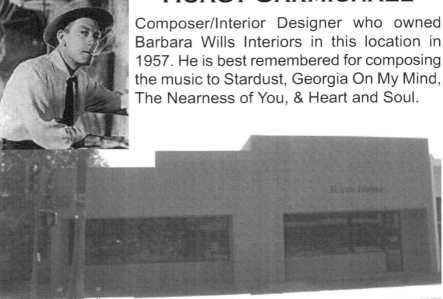

Composer/Interior Designer who owned Barbara Wills Interiors in this location in 1957. He is best remembered for composing the music to Stardust, Georgia On My Mind, The Nearness of You, & Heart and Soul.

AJ 1101 North Palm Canyon Drive
DON THE BEACHCOMBER

Hawaiian dinner house that was a celebrity hangout favorite of many celebrities opened in 1953 with the actual street address of 120 Via Lola. Palm fronds and bamboo booths adorned the interior and Tahitian flavorings accented the food. The chain grew to over 20 locations during the owners lifetime, beginning with the original bar in Hollywood. The Palm Springs location finally closed its doors in the early 1980's. Donn Beach, whose real name was Ernest Raymond Beaumont Gantt, died in 1989 having patented over 80 drinks, mostly with Rum. One of which was the Navy Grog, Frank Sinatra's favorite here in the Tiki Lounge at the Palm Springs Don the Beachcomber. The building has gone through a significant remodel since the hey days of the famous restaurant.

591 North Patencio Road

HERBERT F. JOHNSON, JR.

Grandson of S.C. Johnson & son, who built a cleaning supply empire out of a parquet flooring sales job. Jr. owned the home from 1948-1954. At only 28, his father died and Jr. found himself President of the $5mil company.

GEORGE HAMILTON

1970's home of the vampiric leading man. It was built in 1937 on a 23,087sf lot. Hamilton left his signature in the cement on the right hand side of the driveway.

 ## 701 North Patencio Road

MARY PICKFORD & BUDDY ROGERS

The former home of the silver screen stars (289 titles combined) who were married from 1937 till Pickford's death in 1979. It has 4 bdrms 5 baths and 3,486sf on a 22,216sf lot. The Pickford Theatre in Cathedral City is named in her honor.

AM 784 North Patencio Road
MARIO LANZA

Singer rented this 7 bed 8 bath 1934 home in 1951 to lose 50 pounds & again in 1955. He died four years later at the youthful age of 38. The house has 5,434sf on a 32,670sf llot with a pool and a tennis court.

BETTE DAVIS

Rumors of Davis owning this home could not be verified, although she was known on at least one occasion to share a suite at the Racquet Club with actress Joan Crawford.

AN 975 North Patencio Road
BOB & EILEEN "MIKE" POLLOCK

Creators, writers and Producers of Dynasty, starring John Forsythe, Linda Evans and Joan Collins, bought this 4 bed 4 bath 3,380sf home in 1991 and still own it. The home was built on a 16,553sf lot with a pool in 1977.

AO ## 990 North Patencio Road
HAROLD ROBBINS

Bestselling author of sex riddled romance novels often about Hollywood, Robbins lived in this 4,558sf 6 bed 8 bath 1977 home with his second wife, Grace, till he married his assistant Jann in 1992. After which they moved over to West Camino Sur.

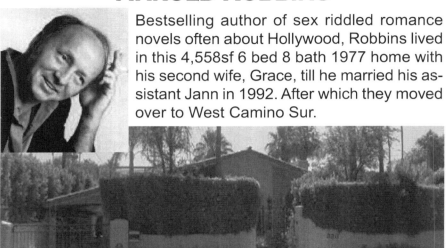

AP ## 993 North Patencio Road
JEANETTE EDRIS

Wife of Arkansas Governor Winthrop Rockefeller owned this home from 1989-1996. It was built in 1957 with 4 bedrooms 4 baths, 4,658 and a pool on a 17,860sf lot. Rockefeller was her fourth husband. They married in 1956 and divorced shortly after he left Governorship in 1971. Edris died in PS.

AQ 999 North Patencio Road

EDWARD G. ROBINSON

Gangster actor's home was designed by A. Quincy Jones and built in 1959. It has 3 bedrooms and 6 baths with 6,307sf and a 44,431sf lot with a pool. Robinson made 101 films in 50 years but after playing Rico in *Little Caesar*(1931) found his niche playing tough guys. He died on Jan. 26, 1973.

AR 735 North Prescott Drive

KIRK KERKORIAN

Multi-billionaire who bought the Flamingo, became President of MGM, merged it with United Artists and opened MGM Grand in Las Vegas bought this 12,510sf 5 bed 8 bath home in 1970. It was built in 1936 and sits on a 40,946sf lot.

AS 875 North Prescott Drive

ROBERT LIPPERT, SR.

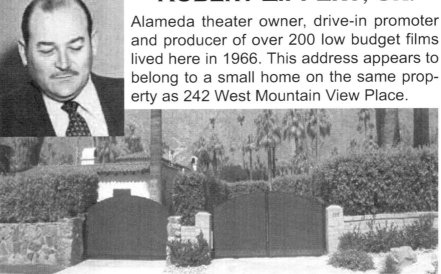

Alameda theater owner, drive-in promoter and producer of over 200 low budget films lived here in 1966. This address appears to belong to a small home on the same property as 242 West Mountain View Place.

AT 1055 North Rose Avenue

JACKIE COOPER

Owner Jackie Cooper moved into this home in 1962. It was built in 1961 with 4 bedrooms 4 baths and 2,799sf on a 12,632sf lot with a pool. During this time, Cooper's career was limited to TV appearances: *Twilight Zone, Danny Kaye Show*, more, till landing the role of Perry White in *Superman*(1978) with Christopher Reeves.

AU ## 1258 North Rose Avenue
NAT "KING" COLE

Cole's ownership of this home could not be verified nor if his daughter Natalie lived here. He was known to stay with Chi-Chi Club owner Irwin Schuman at 201 Camino Norte when performing at the nightclub.

AV ## 1276 North Rose Avenue
ROBERT SURTEES

Veteran cameraman who won three Oscars lived in this 4 bed 3 bath 2,560sf 1962 home on a 13,068sf lot in 1967. He began as an assistant cameraman with Universal in 1927. His work includes: *Thirty Seconds Over Tokyo*(1944), *Oklahoma*(1955), *Ben Hur*(1959), and *The Sting*(1973).

1293 North Rose Avenue

MAURICE MCDONALD

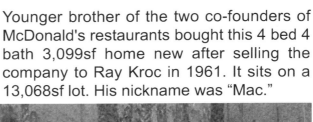

Younger brother of the two co-founders of McDonald's restaurants bought this 4 bed 4 bath 3,099sf home new after selling the company to Ray Kroc in 1961. It sits on a 13,068sf lot. His nickname was "Mac."

1294 North Rose Avenue

SIDNEY SHELDON

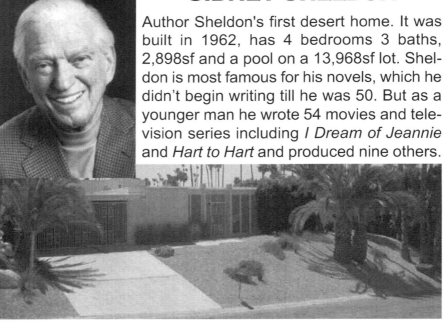

Author Sheldon's first desert home. It was built in 1962, has 4 bedrooms 3 baths, 2,898sf and a pool on a 13,968sf lot. Sheldon is most famous for his novels, which he didn't begin writing till he was 50. But as a younger man he wrote 54 movies and television series including *I Dream of Jeannie* and *Hart to Hart* and produced nine others.

1326 North Rose Avenue
MARILYN MONROE

Reports of Marilyn Monroe renting this 4 bed 3 bath 2,978sf 1961 home, though un-verifed, feel true. I also trace her to The Racquet Club in the '40's and PS photo shoots in '47 & '54, plus the Kennedy affair that happened at Bing Crosby's house.

823 North Topaz Circle
TOMMY & JANIE DORSEY

Brother to big band leader Jimmy Dorsey. Tommy was a band leader and trumpeter in his own right. His widow Janie bought this 1961 4 bedroom, 3 bath home in 1967. It has 2,238sf on a 10,019sf lot.

BA 969 North Tuxedo Circle

GEORGE "BULLETS" DURGOM

Agent to Jackie Gleason, Frank Sinatra, Sammy Davis Jr., Mickey Rooney, Merv Griffin, and more lived here in 1972. The 3 bed/2 bath home was built in 1959 with 1,600sf on a 12,197sf lot. Bullets got his start in entertainment as a road manager for the Glenn Miller band. He died in Palm Desert in 1992.

BB 997 North Tuxedo Circle

BRUNO BERNARD

Photographer, Bernard of Hollywood owned this 3 bed 2 bath home until 1991 when he gave it to his busty Playboy model daughter Susan Lynn Bernard Sommer. She owned it till 2000. It was built in 1959 with 1,600sf on a 13,939sf lot. He also had a photography studio business downtown Palm Springs next to what is now Peabody's Coffee House.

BC 230 North Via Las Palmas West
HARRY WEISS

L.os Angeles criminal defense attorney for Mae West and other celebrities owned this home from 1981-1995. It was built in 1954 with 4 bedrooms and 4 baths, 2,740sf and sits on a 15,682sf lot with a pool.

BD 296 North Via Las Palmas West
IRVING "SWIFTY" LAZAR

Mega-star agent to Cole Porter, Noel Coward, Neil Simon, John Huston, Lauren Bacall, Kirk Douglas, Joan Collins, and more lived here in 1967. The home has 3 bedrooms 3 bath with 2,160sf of living space on a 14,810sf lot. He earned the nickname "Swifty" after putting together three deals for Humphrey Bogart in one day.

BE 610 North Via Monte Vista

PHIL REGAN

New York cop turned actor in the 1930's bought this 4 bedroom 5 bath 3,172sf 1937 home in 1939. Regan acted in 27 titles including *Manhattan Merry-Go-Round*(1937) and *Las Vegas Nights*(1941).

BF 665 North Via Monte Vista

GEORGE LIBERACE

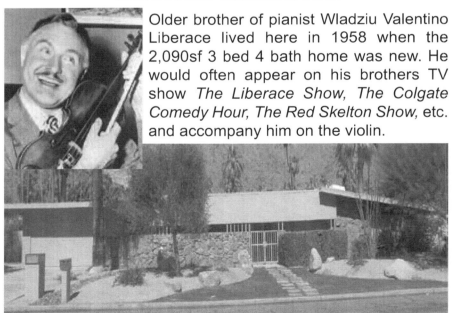

Older brother of pianist Wladziu Valentino Liberace lived here in 1958 when the 2,090sf 3 bed 4 bath home was new. He would often appear on his brothers TV show *The Liberace Show, The Colgate Comedy Hour, The Red Skelton Show*, etc. and accompany him on the violin.

BG 979 North Via Monte Vista
GABE KAPLAN

Welcome Back Kotter star spent some of his TV earnings on this home in the 1970's. It's a 1959 5 bed/3 bath 2,488sf house with a pool on a 10,890sf lot. In March 2005, Kaplan came in 3rd in the World Poker Tour Event at The Mirage in Vegas.

BH 1123 North Via Monte Vista
DEAN & JEANNE MARTIN

Actor, singer, and suave #1 partner of Sinatra's Rat Pack bought this 4 bed 3 bath 2,145sf 1957 home in 1968, and then gave it to Jeanne in their divorce in 1973. He died in 1995. Jeanne still owns it as part of the Jeanne Martin Family Trust.

BI 1295 North Via Monte Vista

PETER LAWFORD

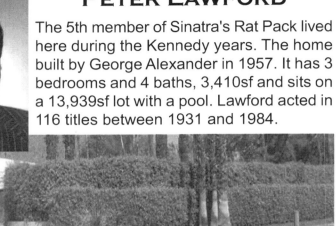

The 5th member of Sinatra's Rat Pack lived here during the Kennedy years. The home built by George Alexander in 1957. It has 3 bedrooms and 4 baths, 3,410sf and sits on a 13,939sf lot with a pool. Lawford acted in 116 titles between 1931 and 1984.

BJ 1303 North Via Monte Vista

SAMMY CAHN

Lyricist/composer bought this 4 bed 3 bath 2,134sf home new in 1957. Cahn won multiple awards for his music including: All the Way (Academy Award, 1957), Three Coins in the Fountain (Academy Award, 1954), Love and Marriage (Emmy Award, 1955), and many more.

BK ## 1575 North Via Norte
EDGAR BERGEN

Ventriloquist/radio/actor and father to Candice Bergen, lived at this address from 1947-1951. Conflicting histories surround this home. It either had a significant remodel in the 1950's or 60's or it was completely torn down & rebuilt.

RUTH TAYLOR

Silent film actress, who played opposite Babe Ruth in Ruth's biopic *Heading Home* in 1920, lived in this 1967 home with 4 bedrooms 4 baths and 3,098sf on a 14,810sf lot in 1975.

BL ## 289 South Via Las Palmas West
JAMES GALANOS

Fashion Designer, who made presidential ball dresses for Nancy Reagan and other celebrities, bought this 4 bedroom, 4 bath, 3,085sf, 1946 home in 1994.

357 South Via Las Palmas West

RONA BARRETT

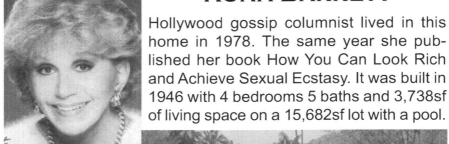

Hollywood gossip columnist lived in this home in 1978. The same year she published her book How You Can Look Rich and Achieve Sexual Ecstasy. It was built in 1946 with 4 bedrooms 5 baths and 3,738sf of living space on a 15,682sf lot with a pool.

425 South Via Las Palmas West

DAVIS FACTOR

Cosmetics Manufacturer and oldest son of Max Factor lived in this 3 bed 5 bath 1946 home in 1959. He ran the Max Factor empire from 1938, when Max died, to 1972, when he sold the company. Davis died in 1991. The home has since been torn down and only the front fence remains.

BO ## 444 North Via Las Palmas West
JERRY HERMAN

Broadway Composer of *Hello Dolly*(1964), *Mame*(1966), *La Cage Aux Folles*(1983), and more, owned this 1981 home from 1999-2004. It has 4 beds 5 baths 4,644sf, a pool and sits on a 16,988sf lot.

BP ## 700 Via Las Palmas West
DONALD O'CONNOR

One of two homes owned by the star of *Singing in the Rain*(1952), *Francis the Talking Mule* (seven movies total from 1950-56), and many more. O'Connor acted in 84 projects throughout his career. This 4 bed 5 bath home was built in 1959 with 2,598sf on a 14,810sf lot.

BQ 840 Via Las Palmas West

DONALD O'CONNOR

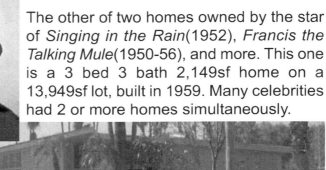

The other of two homes owned by the star of *Singing in the Rain*(1952), *Francis the Talking Mule*(1950-56), and more. This one is a 3 bed 3 bath 2,149sf home on a 13,949sf lot, built in 1959. Many celebrities had 2 or more homes simultaneously.

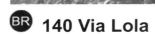

BR 140 Via Lola

SUNSET TOWER APARTMENTS

Hotel and apartments, built in 1956 at the doorway adjoining the Las Palmas neighborhood to downtown Palm Springs, leased rooms to many celebrities.

BT 1455 Vine Avenue
HOWARD HAWKS

Director of *The Outlaw* starring Jane Russell and produced by Howard Hughes. The 5 bedroom 5 bath home is called "Casa De Plata." and is the same as 501 Stevens Road but from a different entrance. It was built in 1949 with 5,131sf on a 27,878sf lot. Hawks lived here for 30 years till his death in 1977.

BU 1166 Via Vespero North
"COLONEL" TOM PARKER

Elvis Presley's manager owned this 4 bed 3 bath 2,616sf 1957 home in the 1970's during Elvis's reign as The King of Vegas. The title then becomes vague as to ownership. But in 1987 the William Morris Agency sold the home on a clear title.

1200 Via Vespero North

ROSIE DOLLY

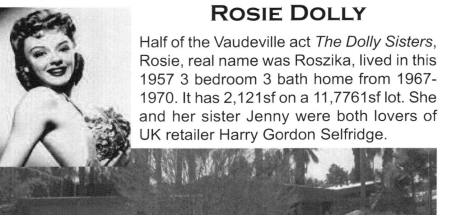

Half of the Vaudeville act *The Dolly Sisters*, Rosie, real name was Roszika, lived in this 1957 3 bedroom 3 bath home from 1967-1970. It has 2,121sf on a 11,7761sf lot. She and her sister Jenny were both lovers of UK retailer Harry Gordon Selfridge.

 1254 Via Vespero North

MILTON PRELL

Founder of The Sahara and owner of The Aladdin also owned this 3,021sf 5 bed 4 bath home, built in 1957 on a 12,197sf home. Prell was a known friend of Colonel Tom Parker and when Elvis and Priscilla fled PS in Sinatra's plane, it was to Prell's private suite at the Aladdin where they wed.

274 West Alejo Road
FRANCES ZUCHOWSKI

Mother to the famed pianist Liberace, lived here next to her son, till her death in 1980. A simple title search revealed no records found on this home, indicating to the author that at some point in the past the address had been changed.

226 West Alejo Road/501 North Belardo Road
ALVAH HICKS

(Renumbered 501 North Belardo Road) Hicks built this home in 1930 and called it "Villa Teresa" after his wife. Hicks and his family lived here till 1936. They owned Palm Springs Water Company, subdivided the land for the development of the Las Palmas neighborhood and built about twenty homes in the area and Our Lady of Solitude Church across the street.

Wealthy Reno, Nevada socialite **Ludovica Dimon Graham** owned this home from 1936-1945. Ludovica's family maintained homes in San Francisco, Boston and New York and had a long history of building American Clipper ships in the 19th century.

226 W. Alejo Rd./501 N. Belardo Rd. Continued...

The retired commercial furrier, **Walter Glatter**, bought this home from 1945-1960.

MURIEL FULTON

Fulton, a local realtor bought this home in 1960 intending to turn it into a hotel and hired Spanish Revivalist architect Walter Neff who helped change it from an expansive home into a business with multiple suites and private patios. At this time the home was renamed "The Cloisters" and the address was changed to 501 North Belardo Road. The hotel though, never caught on.

WLADZIU VALENTINO LIBERACE

The famed pianists' most famous Palm Springs home. His friends called him Lee and he owned this home from 1967-1987. He renamed the home "Casa De Liberace." After remodel after remodel over the years it is now a 5 bedroom 7 bath home with 6,094sf, a fountain and a pool on a 25,700sf lot. He owned five homes total in Palm Springs, including his mothers.

 357 West Camino Sur

SOL LESSER

Tarzan Producer lived in this 4 bed/4 bath home in 1947. It was built in 1946 with 2,952sf of space on a 16,117sf lot. This home was also the scene of a 1952 jewelry heist.

CB 377 West Camino Sur

DONALD WILLS DOUGLAS, SR.

Founder of Douglas Aircraft owned this home till he died in 1981. It was built in 1954 with 5 bedrooms and 5 baths, 3,689sf of living space, a pool and sits on a 16,553sf lot.

CC 523 West Camino Sur

ADOLPHE MENJOU

Actor who played Attorney Billy Flynn in Roxie Hart which inspired the play and film Chicago. He acted in 149 projects, nearly all movies, including: *The Sheik*(1921), *A Farewell to Arms*(1932), *Science Fiction Theatre*(TV/1955), and more. Menjou lived here in 1946. The home was built in 1936 with 2,639sf & 4 bedrooms and 5 baths.

CD 550 West Camino Sur

GEORGE & ROSALIE HEARST

Rosalie inherited this 4 bed 5 bath 5,698sf home in 1972 from George and lived here till 1999. It was built in 1963 on a 23,522sf lot. The Rosalie Hearst Trust owned it till 2001.

CE 601 West Camino Sur

HAROLD ROBBINS

Best selling author lived in this 4 bed 4 bath 4,000sf 1958 home on a 15,246sf lot with a pool, with his third wife Jann till his death in 1997. Jann sold it in 1999.

Harold is the only person I ever met with a real Picasso on his wall; a portrait of Robbins himself which Picasso gave to him after sharing the same dog walking route in Paris years earlier. Harold was a foul-mouthed son of a gun who would pay his New York Times delivery bill to my Dad by having me come over to his house to sign 50-100 books every few months.

CF 697 West Camino Sur

CYD CHARISSE & TONY MARTIN

Nightclub entertainer/husband Martin (*Ziegfeld Girl*, 1941) and Ballet dancer/wife Charisse (*Singin' in the Rain*, 1952) moved into this home when it was brand new in 1958 and raised two sons here. It has 4 bedrooms and 3 baths, 2,534sf, a pool and sits on a 12,632sf lot.

CG 740 West Camino Sur

KIM NOVAK

Novak rented this home in the late 1960's. It was built in 1958 with 4 bedrooms and 4 baths in 2,553sf on a 13,068sf lot. She began her career as an extra in *Veil of Baghdad*(1953) and one of her more recent roles was as Kit Marlowe in *Falcon Crest*(1987).

893 West Camino Sur

GEORGE ARNOLD

Producer of Rhythm on Ice bought this home when it was new in 1961. It has 3,608sf, 3 bdms and 4 baths on a 17,424sf lot.

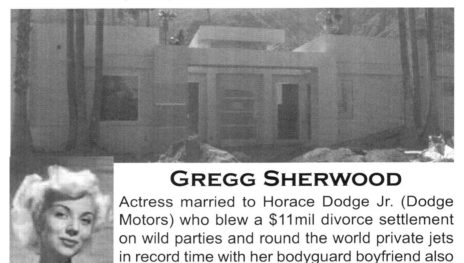

GREGG SHERWOOD

Actress married to Horace Dodge Jr. (Dodge Motors) who blew a $11mil divorce settlement on wild parties and round the world private jets in record time with her bodyguard boyfriend also lived in this home till 1977.

MURDER-ROBBERY

In 1978, this home was the site of Palm Springs first triple homicide murder when a local realtor, staying here at the time, with his wife and their maid were all three shot execution style in connection with a robbery.

GEORGE NADER

Gay actor (69 roles from 1950-74), Sci-Fi author (Chrome, 1987) and boyfriend of Rock Hudson lived here from 1991 till his death in 2002.

CI 460 West Canyon Place
ROBERT HANSON

Playboy son of British industrialist Lord Hanson bought this 6 bed 6 bath home in 1991. It was built in 1982 with 4,748sf, a four car garage, a pool and a tennis court on a 64,033sf lot.

CK 222 West Chino Drive
SAMMY DAVIS, JR.

Sammy purportedly rented this 3 bed 4 bath 3,301sf home, built in 1925 on a 26,136sf lot with a pool, although it could not be verified.

CLARK GABLE & CAROLE LOMBARD

Three stories of these silver screen legends surround this house. One: it was owned by the couple during their married years of 1939-1942 and another is that Gable rented this home and then moved to Bermuda Dunes CC just before his death in 1960. No evidence to support either story has yet been found. Also, Kay Spreckles Gable, former wife of Clark Gable from 1955-60 is supposed to have owned this home. While still un-verified this seems the most likely history of this property.

CL 1111 West Dolores Court

RUTA LEE

Lee has lived in this 2,471sf 3 bed 2 bath home on a 10,454sf lot since 1995. She began her career in 1953 by playing a teenager in *The Adventures of Superman* & has acted in 147 titles since including: *Three's Company*(1979 & '82), *Charles in Charge*(1990) and her upcoming film *For Better or For Worse*(2013).

CM 261 West Hermosa Place

JAMES DARCIE LLOYD

Father of actor Harold Lloyd lived here until his death in 1947. The 3 bedroom 5 bath home was built in 1937 with 3,803sf on a 25,700sf lot with a pool.

CN 296 West Hermosa Place

LEW WASSERMAN

Music Corporation of America Chairman Emeritus bought this 5 bed 4 bath 1957 home in 1960. Designed by Harold Levitt. It has 4,080sf on a 24,394sf lot. While Wasserman was a strong player in the Democratic party, he was instrumental in helping Ronald Reagan to become President of the Screen Actor's Guild.

CO 334 West Hermosa Place

SAMUEL GOLDWYN

It seems the studio chief owned this home for a number of years, estimated from the late 1940's till 1960, and either rented or loaned it out to those he wanted to woo into his stable of stars or as a reward for those he wanted to keep.

334 West Hermosa Place Continued...

334 West Hermosa Place Continued...

EDMUND GOULDING

British director of Bette Davis (*Dark Victory*, 1939-an MGM priductions) and Tyrone Power (*The Razor's Edge*, 1946 and *Nightmare Alley*, 1947), who rented this home in 1950. At the time, Goulding was working primarily as a director for 20th Century Fox.

LUCILLE BALL & DESI ARNAZ

In 1954, the famous couple were listed under this address in the Palm Springs White Pages. They took this more semi-permanent step to oversee construction of their Thunderbird Ranch home in Rancho Mirage which was completed later that same year. In years to come, Desi and his Orchestra would open the Chi Chi Club & Lucy hosted the Desert Circus Parade.

JUDY GARLAND

In 1955, the actress rented 1045 North Cahuilla Road, which shares the property with 334 west Hermosa Place. Most likely, either Goldwyn or some other owner has since joined the two properties. Garland signed with MGM in 1938 and in the fall of 1954 she released *A Star Is Born*.

SEYMOUR LAZAR

Entertainment lawyer and his wife Alyce have owned this home since at least 1981, along with several other homes in the Palm Springs area. Lazar has had many famous clients including: Woody Allen, Sidney Sheldon, Lenny Bruce, the Beatles and more. In January of 2008, Lazar was convicted in a Los Angeles court of illegal kickbacks involving a class action court scheme.

CP ## 369 West Hermosa Place

JANE WYMAN

Wyman moved into this home after divorcing Ronald Reagan in 1948. The 5 bed 5 bath 4,763sf home was built in 1952 on a 31,363sf lot with a pool.

CQ ## 417 West Hermosa Place

LEO SPITZ

President of Universal-International Pictures owned this 1937 home from 1950-1956.

ELIZABETH TAYLOR & MICHAEL TODD

In 1957, the star of *Giant*(1956), *National Velvet*(1944) & more, and her newlywed husband, the inventor of Todd-O, a high definition wide screen process rented this gigantic home on a 65,776sf lot.

CR 432 West Hermosa Place

JERRY HERMAN

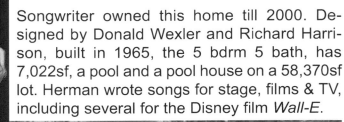

Songwriter owned this home till 2000. Designed by Donald Wexler and Richard Harrison, built in 1965, the 5 bdrm 5 bath, has 7,022sf, a pool and a pool house on a 58,370sf lot. Herman wrote songs for stage, films & TV, including several for the Disney film *Wall-E*.

CT 494 West Hermosa Place

ZADDIE BUNKER

Palm Springs pioneer who moved to the desert in 1914 to live in a lean-to and after her husband left her became the area's first female auto mechanic, lived here in 1965. She also was California's first female licensed chauffeur and eventually became known as the flying great-grandmother.

©️ 457 West Hermosa Place

DONALD DUNCAN

Owner of Duncan Toys/Duncan YoYo. Mis-credited as inventor of the Yoyo (See wikipedia) lived in this home in 1951. The home has 6 bed 8 bath 7,715sf and was built in 1928 on a massive 172,498sf lot.

ANN MILLER & ARTHUR CAMERON

Texas Oilman Arthur Cameron lived with actress Ann Miller here in 1958. She married his brother George. Arthur bought this home prior to Duncan's death in 1971. Miller had acted in lots of films by this time, including *Easter Parade*(1948) and *Kiss Me Kate*(1953), and many more. She continued acting all through her life, with appearances on *Love American Style*(1972), *The Love Boat*(1982) and *Home Improvement*(1992). She died in 2004 of lung cancer only a few years after her last role as Coco in *Mulholland Drive*(2001).

TONI HOLT

KTLA-TV *Talk of the Town* personality has owned this home with her car dealer husband Robert Kramer since 1995.

ⓒ**ⓤ 271 West Merito Place**

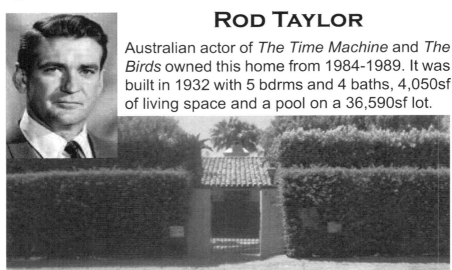

ROD TAYLOR

Australian actor of *The Time Machine* and *The Birds* owned this home from 1984-1989. It was built in 1932 with 5 bdrms and 4 baths, 4,050sf of living space and a pool on a 36,590sf lot.

GEORGE ROSENTHAL

Owner of Raleigh Studios, the largest independent studio operator in the U.S., bought this home in 1989 and owned it till 1996.

ⓒ**ⓥ 300 West Merito Place**

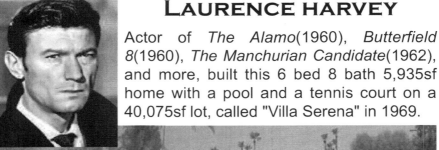

LAURENCE HARVEY

Actor of *The Alamo*(1960), *Butterfield 8*(1960), *The Manchurian Candidate*(1962), and more, built this 6 bed 8 bath 5,935sf home with a pool and a tennis court on a 40,075sf lot, called "Villa Serena" in 1969.

(CW) 348 West Merito Place
CLAUDE BINYON

Journalist, writer, director stayed here in 1939, two years after it was built. It has 4,050sf with 5 bdrm/6 bath and was owned by clothiers William & Iris Wardlaw.

GREG NIEMANN

Author of Palm Springs Legends, Las Vegas Legends, Baja Legends and Big Brown: The Untold Story of UPS, Niemann and his wife Leila purchased this home in 2004 and still live here.

(CX) 443 West Merito Place
LILY TOMLIN

Actress who played the nasally telephone operator on *Laugh-in*(1970-73) and starred in *9 to 5*(1980), *All of Me*(1984), and more, owned this home from 1997-2003. It was built in 1952 with 3 bedrooms 6 baths, 4,854sf and a pool on a 24,394sf lot.

CY **465 West Merito Place**

LENA HORNE

Civil Rights Activist and black actress, Horne, bought this 3 bed 4 bath home originally under an assumed name in the late 1950's at the height of her career. It was built in 1956 with 3,869sf on a 24,829sf lot with a pool. In 1958, she was nominated for a Tony award for her Broadway role in *Jamaica*.

CZ **478 West Merito Place**

WILLIAM GARGAN

Oscar nominated actor who later in life lost his larynx due to throat cancer lived here with his wife Mary Kenny in 1940. He named his autobiography Why Me? The 4 bed 5 bath home was built in 1937 with 5,012sf on a 26,572sf corner lot.

DA ## 481 West Merito Place

HOOT GIBSON

Western actor who became a top real estate agent in the desert built this home in 1936. It has 5 bedrooms 4 baths, 5,536sf on a 28,314sf lot. Gibson started in silent films, beginning with *Pride fo the Range*(1910) and then moved to talkies. His last role was as a roadblock deputy in *Ocean's Eleven*(1960) with The Rat Pack.

DB ## 242 West Mountain View Place

CARL LYKKEN

Palm Springs first Postmaster, store owner and owner of the city's first telephone lived here in 1946. The home is actually 3 properties joined together (242 Mountain View + 375 & 385 Prescott Drive) with six structures: 2 full size homes, 2 guest cottages, a four car garage and a pool house, with a pool of course. The original structure was built in 1930 with 4,090sf, 4 bdrms 4 bath, on a 23,087sf lot. His name is pronounced Licken.

DC 325 West Mountain View Place

HOMER CURRAN

San Francisco stage producer and owner of the Cort and Curran Theatres, lived here shortly before dying in 1952 when the home was first built. It's a 6 bed 7 bath, 5,100sf house on a 37,897sf lot. Curran also founded the San Francisco Light Opera Company and co-authored operetta books.

DD 328 West Mountain View Place

EDDIE LEBARON

Bandleader and actor lived here in the 1950's. LeBaron, was a classy music man, with a great house, who had a mild acting career, 21 roles between 1944-63, where he usually played small parts or portrayed himself as in *Casa Manana*(1951).

328 West Mountain View Place continues...

328 West Mountain View Place continued...
IRVING P. KRICK

Meterologist who helped predict the right day to burn Atlanta in *Gone With the Wind* and selected the invasion date of Allied Forces D-Day, June 6, 1944, for ideal weather conditions. Krick owned here in 1974 when it was invaded by mask wearing robbers who pistol whipped his 23 year old son and sexually assaulted his wife during a home invasion.

GLEN A. LARSON

Writer and TV-Producer of such famous prime-time hits: *Battlestar Galactica* (both the 1978 original and the 2004 Sci-Fi channel remake), *Knight Rider* starring David Hasselhoff, *Magnum P.I.* starring Tom Selleck, *The Fall Guy* starring Lee Majors, PS I Love U, and many many more, purchased this home in 1983.

GENE AUTRY

Final Palm Springs resting place of Gene Autry who bought the 10,587sf 5 bed 5 bath home in 1997. The home, built in 1940, has a 6 car garage, a tennis court and a pool on a 61,855sf lot. Autry has a long history in the city of Palm Springs including, the ownership of the Gene Autry Hotel and the bringing of the Anaheim Angels baseball team to the desert for their spring training in the 1960's and 70's to Angel Stadium in Sunrise Park.

125

DE 247 West Stevens Road

SAMMY SHORE

La Siesta Villas, ran by comedian Sammy Shore in 1982. The hotel was designed by Albert Frey and built in 1965 as a collection of 1 and 2 bedroom villas. Shore, was the opening act for Elvis at The Hilton International in Las Vegas from 1969-72. He also founded The Comedy Store.

DF 368 West Stevens Road

CAROLYN JONES

Best known for playing Morticia on *The Addams Family*. Her other works include: *How the West Was Won*(1962), *Batman*(1966-67) as Marsha, Queen of Diamonds, and many more. Jones lived in this 3 bed 3 bath 1,918sf home with her husband, assistant director Herbert Greene, in 1974. It was built in 1945 on a 13,405sf lot.

DG ## 591 West Stevens Road
HARRY WARNER

Oldest of the four Warner Brothers (others: Sam, Jack, & Albert) owned here in 1957 for only a year because he died. His daughter Doris Warner inherited it and lived here the rest of her life till 1978. The 5,308sf home was built in 1937 with 9 bedrooms and 9 baths on a 27,443sf lot.

DH ## 670 West Stevens Road
DEBBIE REYNOLDS

While living here in the 1960's, actress Reynolds made *How The West Was Won* and *The Unsinkable Molly Brown* and was married to shoe mogul and high stakes gambler Harry Karl. The home was designed by Howard Lapham and built in 1957 with 4 bedrooms and 5 baths in 5,560sf atop a 24,829sf lot.

DI 695 West Stevens Road

JOHN PHILLIPS

Leader of the sixties folk group The Mamas and the Papas owned this 3 bed 4 bath home from 1995-2001. It was built in 1957 with 3,413sf on a 20,473sf lot.

LEO SPITZ & ELEANOR ROOSEVELT

President of Universal-International Pictures entertained former first lady Eleanor Roosevelt here in 1960.

DJ 484 West Vereda Sur/475 Via Las Palmas West

RUDY VALLEE

Crooner & Actor owned a home here from 1946-1957. But the home was torn down for the construction of this new one at 475 South Via Las Palmas in 1992. Vallee began his career as a sax player, then became a band leader, switched to radio and movies. He was known as a slave driving man to work for.

(DK) ## 248 West Vereda Norte

KLARA MACNEE & STEVE SEKELY

Klara Sekely Macnee (Baba Majos de Nagyzsenye) is now married to Avengers actor Patrick Macnee (active nudist). While owning this home, MacNee's third wife was married to Steve Sekely, Director of *Revenge of the Zombies* and *The Day of the Triffids* until his death in 1979. Klara owned this 3 bed 3 bath 2,801sf 1952 home till 1993 & she lost it in another divorce.

(DL) ## 383 West Vereda Norte

WILLIAM & "MOUSIE" POWELL

Home is designated Historic Site #28 and built in 1935-36. Powell was a leading man who acted in 94 titles between 1922-55 and Mousie was in 19 titles from 1934-43. In many ways, they were the Premier and First Lady of Palm Springs. Actor & his wife (real name: Diana Lewis) owned this 6 bed 6 bath home from 1941-1984. It has 4,999sf on a 18,295sf lot.

DM 321 West Vereda Sur

EDDIE LEBARON

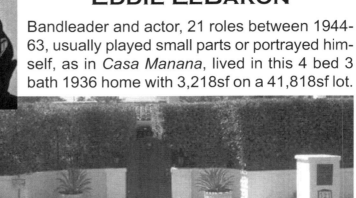

Bandleader and actor, 21 roles between 1944-63, usually played small parts or portrayed himself, as in *Casa Manana*, lived in this 4 bed 3 bath 1936 home with 3,218sf on a 41,818sf lot.

DN 285 West Via Lola

JACK L. WARNER

Co-founder and the driving force Warner Brothers Pictures, who took it from his brothers in a hostile takeover, built this home in 1958 and named it the same as his home on the French riviera"Villa Aujourd Hui." It's a 6 bedroom 6 bath home with 4,421sf and a pool on a 23,958sf lot.

STEPHEN SHAGAN

Crime novelist and Oscar nominee for *Save the Tiger*(1974), owned this home from 1990-2004. He wrote his first novel on a typewriter loaned to him by author Harold Robbins..

350 West Via Lola

BRIAN FOY

Eldest son of the Vaudeville act *The Seven little Foys*, who became a director-producer of 255 films, including Ronald Reagan movies lived here in 1946. The home is 4 bed 5 bath 4,780sf, built in 1962 on a 16,117sf lot

375 West Via Lola

ANDREA LEEDS

Actress married to Robert Howard, whose father owned the racehorse Seabiscuit lived here with their children. In 1960, their nineteen year old son, Robert Jr., was bit by a rattlesnake for the third time in the backyard and nearly died. The rattlesnake was a pet. The 1954 home is a 4 bed 5 bath house with 3,777sf & a 17,860sf lot.

SIDNEY SHELDON

Author Sheldon's fourth desert home. He bought it in 1994 with his second wife Alexandra Kostoff. He owned three PS homes side by side of each other. This one is still owned by Alexandra.

DR 425 West Via Lola

SIDNEY SHELDON

Author Sheldon and wife's Alexandra Kostoff second desert home. He bought it in 1977. He owned three homes side by side of each other. This one was built in 1959, has 6 bed 7 baths, 7,370sf, a pool, and sits on a 27,007sf lot.

DT 515 West Via Lola

KIRK DOUGLAS

Second Palm Springs home of Douglas who lived here with his second wife, Anne Buydens, in 1957. It was designed by Donald Wexler and built in 1954. It has 5 bedrooms and 5 baths in 3,790sf of interior space on a 32,670sf lot with a pool and a tennis court.

HEPBURN & TRACY

Katherine Hepburn stayed here with Spencer Tracy while making *It's a Mad, Mad, Mad World* in 1963 when home was owned by Douglas.

DS 467 West Via Lola

KITTY CARLISLE

Kitty and her husband Moss Hart, Broadway director of *Camelot* and *My Fair Lady,* lived here in 1961, when Moss died of a heart attack on the front lawn of their 42,689sf lot where their 8 bedroom 11 bath, 7,131sf 1948 home sat. Carlisle was a star of theatre, film and TV, best known as a panelist on *To Tell The Truth.*

WINTHROP ROCKEFELLER

Governor of Arkansas and a son of John D. Rockefeller purchased this home from Moss Hart's widow, Kitty Carlisle, in 1963. During Winthrop's term as Governor ('66-70) he racially integrated the schools, established a Human Relations Council and appointed African Americans to the Draft Boards.

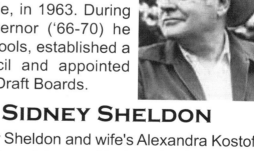

SIDNEY SHELDON

Author Sheldon and wife's Alexandra Kostoff third desert home. He bought this one in 1992. Alexandra still owns it too. The backyards to all three have connecting gates so visiting family doesn't have to walk onto the street to get together.

DU 535 West Via Lola
SIDNEY KORSHAK

Los Angeles Gangster attorney who defended Al Capone, worked for the Teamsters & was called the most powerful lawyer in the world, bought this 6 bed 4 bath 4,204sf 1951 home in 1976. It sits on a 17,424sf lot. Korshak is the attorney who convinced Barbara Sinatra to sign a pre-nuptial with Old Blue Eyes.

DV 550 West Via Lola
KURT RUSSELL & GOLDIE HAWN

Actor and Actress rented here before buying a permanent desert residence in Bighorn in 2003. This home is a 3 bed 5 bath, 4,400sf, built in 1974 on a 13,939sf lot with a pool. in 1983, Russell and Hawn met on the set of the film *Swing Shift*, one year later they made *Overboard* & have been together ever since.

DW 312 West Via Sol

JACK LATHAM

KNBC-TV News Anchorman & General Manager of KPLM (now KESQ) lived here for 18 years until his death in 1987. The 4 bedroom 3 bath home was built in 1936 with 2,748sf on a 13,068sf lot with a pool.

DX 373 West Via Sol

JASCHA HEIFITZ

Decca & RCA recording artist and one of the greatest violinists of all time, retired to this large 2 bed 2 bath home in 1972. At 16, he told Groucho Marx he'd been playing since six. Groucho jokingly said, "And before that you were just a bum." Heifitz defected from Russia in 1917 and played for the London, Boston, and other symphonies.

DY 483 West Via Sol

CHARLES WALTERS

Director, choreographer, dancer of Fred Astaire and Ginger Rogers & Gene Kelly and Judy Garland, more. Walters built this 4 bed 3 bath home, dubbed "Casa Contenta" in 1956. It has 2,518sf and a pool on a 15,682sf lot.

DZ 827 West Via Vadera

GEORGE HAMILTON

Actor's first desert home. It was built in 1958, has 4 bdrms and 4 baths in 2,561sf of space and sits on a 13,608sf lot with a pool. Hamilton has acted in 105 titles since he began in 1958. One of his earliest roles was on *The Adventures of Rin Tin Tin*(1958), a recent role was on the TV show *Pushing Daisies*(2008).

EA 424 West Vista Chino
TOM & ANITA MAY

Owners, founders of May Company. Built in 1952 by George and Robert Alexander and designed by William F. Cody. This 7 bdrm 6 bath home has 4,946sf, a tennis court and a pool. In 1964, it was redesigned by architect Samuel Marx.

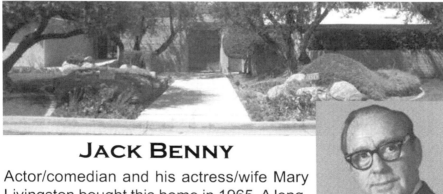

JACK BENNY

Actor/comedian and his actress/wife Mary Livingston bought this home in 1965. A long-time desert fan, Benny lived here till his death in 1974.

EB 470 West Vista Chino
BARRY MANILOW

Designed by Richard Neutra, built in 1946 and called "The Kaufmann House." Singer and songwriter Manilow owned this 4 bdrm 2 bath 3,162sf home with a huge pool and a tennis court from the 1970's till 1993.

1954 Palm Springs Phone Directory Advertisement

Movie Colony & El Mirador Neighborhoods

In 1927, from the moment the El Mirador hotel opened its doors, the formerly windy dunes along Indian Canyon Drive became Palm Springs favorite watering hole and put the City on the map as an elite vacation destination and the celebrities who stayed there soon discovered that a rented room was not enough to satisfy their passion for the desert.

The area I always considered the Movie Colony is but a small section of homes built in the 1930's on the streets squeezed between Indian Canyon Drive and North Miraleste & Tamarisk and Alejo. But the city grows and changes and so do the homewoners who wish to be included in this prisitine selection of homes. So we adapt and accept the larger boundaries set by the Movie Colony and El Mirador neighborhood coalitions which now participate in governance and development; and perhaps rightly so.

While writing this book, I was pleasantly surprised at the quantity and quality of celebrities that encompassed the homes here. Every bit as intriguing as the Las Palmas neighborhood, this section of Palm Springs will delight you for hours on end as you see the numerous hotels, estates and homes of the stars.

The El Mirador hotel itself is gone, replaced by Desert Hospital and still bearing a replica of the famed hotels' bell tower. The original one was kept by the hotel, but unfortunately burnt in a fire in the 1970's.

Ruth Hardy Park, named for the original owner of the Ingleside Inn, has joined the hospital as the hub for this PS area.

139

Movie Colony & El Mirador Neighborhoods

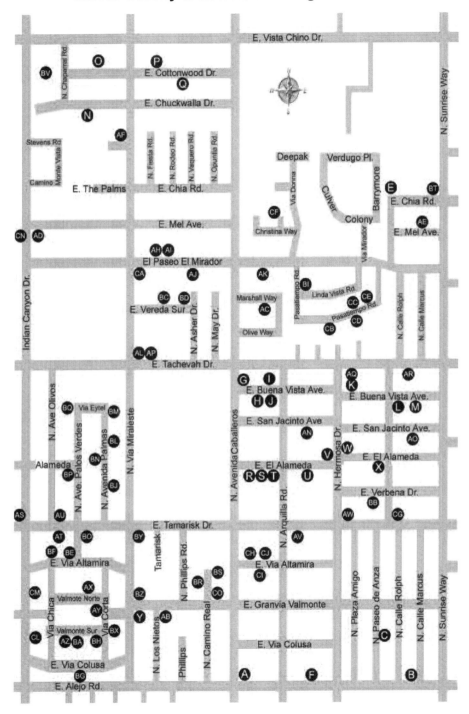

Ⓐ 200 North Avenida Caballeros
CLARA BOW

The home no longer stands but the memory of America's first sweetheart of film lives on. Her time in the desert was spent visiting friends Charles "Buddy" Rogers, Janet Gaynor & Bob Hope. She was listed in the 1959 Palm Springs phone book as living here and when I moved to the desert in 1976 the home was still standing, though in decrepit shape. But somewhere in the 1990's, when the PS Convention Center was expanded, the home was torn down.

Ⓑ 505 North Calle Marcus
MICKEY FINN

Character actor who played cowboys and pirates lived in this small (937sf) 2 bed 2 bath home in 1960. It was built in 1955 and has a 6,534sf lot. Here he is shown from his appearance on *The Rifleman* starring Chuck Connors, another PS resident.

© 550 Paseo De Anza North

BEN POLLACK

Orchestra leader whose band featured such future talents as Glenn Miller, Benny Goodman and Charlie Spivack committed suicide by hanging from the bathroom shower rail of this tiny 839sf 2 bed 2 bath home on June 7th, 1971. It was built in 1951 on a 6,098sf lot.

Ⓔ 1415 Chia Road East

BETTY HUTTON

(Ranch Club Condominiums) Actress, singer, comedienne, lived in these condos in 1999. She was Queen of the Desert Circus Parade in 1954 and rode down Palm Canyon Drive with Grand Marshall Walt Disney, Phil Harris and El Mirador Hotel owner Ray Ryan.

F 1148 East Alejo Road

FRANK SINATRA

(Was 1145 East Via Colusa) Designed by E. Stewart Williams and built in 1947 for $110,000 for the famous crooner, Sinatra lived in this 4 bed 5 bath 3,617sf home with a pool on a 35,017sf lot with first wife Nancy Barbato and then with second wife, Ava Gardner, whom he married in 1951. The story goes that when Frank was mar-ried to Nancy they went out for dinner & drinks at the Chi Chi Club downtown Palm Springs and while dancing the emcee suddenly called for a partners switch and Frank found himself in the arms of Ava Gardner. Sinatra sold the home after his divorce from Ava in 1957.

MOSS HART & JUDY GARLAND

Playwright, Moss, rented this home from Frank Sinatra so he and Judy Garland could work on the rewriting of *A Star Is Born* (1954) after meeting here and sharing ideas during a dinner party.

Ⓖ 1014 East Buena Vista Drive

BOB & DOLORES HOPE

Actor purchased this home in 1941. The 3 bed 3 bath home was built in 1936 with 2,126sf on a 10,019sf lot. They lived here till 1946 when their fourth child necessitated a larger home and they purchased another Palm Springs property on El Alameda. The home is still part of the Dolores Hope Trust.

Ⓗ 1057 East Buena Vista Drive

TOM NEAL

Boxer & actor's second desert home bought in 1964 with his third wife, Gail Evatt. The 3 bed 3 bath 1,874sf home was built in 1964 on a 10,019sf lot. He sold this home and moved to the Little Tuscany area to pay creditors. His marriage suffered and in a rampage, he killed his wife and was convicted of murder in Indio.

I 1062 East Buena Vista Drive
RAOUL WALSH

Built in 1937 with 3 bedrooms and 5 baths with 3,098 of interior space on a 10,019sf lot. It was home to actor/director Walsh of *Thief of Baghdad, High Sierra, The Naked and the Dead*, and many more.

RICHARD HARRISON

Aging actor bought this home with his beautiful young wife Francesca in 1994, ran for Mayor of Palm Springs, lost, and sold it in 2003.

J 1073 East Buena Vista Drive
ROMAN RYTERBAND

Composer, conductor lived here from 1967 till he died in 1979. The home has 2 bedrooms 3 baths, 2,079sf on a 10,019sf lot.

Ⓚ 1248 East Buena Vista Drive

MARJORIE RAMBEAU

Actress who in her youth was underappreciated, but in her maturity became a profound supporting actress. She was nominated for an Oscar twice while playing a prostitute mother opposite Ginger Rogers and then Joan Crawford. She died in this 4 bed 4 bath 3,014sf home on July 7, 1970.

Ⓛ 1411 East Buena Vista Drive

GANT GAITHER

Broadway and Film Producer, author of Grace Kelly: Princess of Monaco, and artist, Gaither lived in this 2,629sf 4 bed 4 bath home on a 10,454sf lot from 1992-2004. He produced *My Six Loves* starring Debbie Reynolds and James Garner and worked on *Winged Victory* with writer Moss Hart.

Ⓜ 1477 East Buena Vista Drive
CHRISTOPHER LEWIS

Director, KWXY disc jockey and son of Loretta Young, lived here from 1988-1999. The 2,325sf 4 bed 3 bath home was built in 1959 on a 10,019sf lot. His first job in TV was manning a warning bell and light to refrain people from talking on the set during the production of his Moms show.

Ⓝ 443 East Chuckawalla Road
MILTON CANIFF

In 1975, cartoonist of realistic strips *Terry and the Pirates & Steve Canyon*, lived here. Caniff also cartooned under the pen name Paul Arthur and received Cartoonist of the Year and Reuben Awards. He was called "the Rembrandt of the comic strip."

🔘 448 East Cottonwood Road

JOHN AGAR

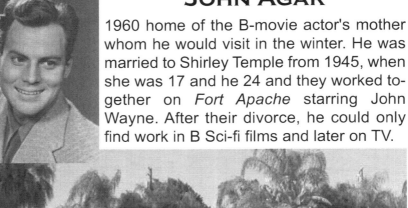

1960 home of the B-movie actor's mother whom he would visit in the winter. He was married to Shirley Temple from 1945, when she was 17 and he 24 and they worked together on *Fort Apache* starring John Wayne. After their divorce, he could only find work in B Sci-fi films and later on TV.

🅿 720 East Cottonwood Road

HENRY TRAVERS

British born actor who played the guardian angel, Clarence Oddbody, in the Frank Capra holiday classic *It's a Wonderful Life*, opposite Jimmy Stewart lived in the Seabrooke Apartments. He was nominated for Best Supporting Actor for playing Mr. Ballard in the WWII film of *Mrs. Miniver* starring Greer Garson.

ⓠ 807 East Cottonwood Road
BEN POLLACK

(Fountain D'Or Apartments) Orchestra leader and Dixieland drummer lived in these apartments in 1966. His band had prominent musicians Glenn Miller and Benny Goodman. In 1971 he hung himself in the bathroom of his other new Palm Springs home.

Ⓡ 1011 East El Alameda (continued on next page...)
BING CROSBY

Bing lived here with his first wife, Dixie Lee, and their sons for 30 something years, well into the 1960's. The 3 bed 3 bath 1934 home has 3,237sf of living space on a 13,068sf lot. These were Bings prime years: comedies with Bob Hope, holiday classics like White Christmas & more.

® 1011 East El Alameda (...continued)

tic adventures like *A Connecticut Yankee in King Arthur's Court* and many more. All in all he acted in 87 shows, did 204 soundtracks, produced 6 projects and released many albums.

MARILYN & JFK

It is claimed that it was under this roof where  President John F. Kennedy and Marilyn Monroe committed adultery. According to Marilyn biographer Donald Spoto, the affair lasted a total of eight years. So it is possible that some of the other locations in the desert which claim to be rendezvous sites of the President and his Hollywood bombshell lover may also be true. After all, it seems entirely plausible that Jack would get together with America's favorite blonde on more than one occasion if he could.

BILL HAMILTON

George Hamilton's younger fashion sensitive brother, Bill, lived here while working at Eva Gabor Interiors at 190 East Palm Canyon Drive in the 1960's and early 1970's.

ROY RANDOLPH

Choreographer and dance instructor lived here for a few years during retirement in the early 1970's. Randolph was a dance teacher to Shirley Temple, Jackie Cooper, Glenn Ford, Betty Grable, Barbara Stanwyck, and more.

ELAYNE VALDEZ

Widow of Cuban band leader Miguelito Valdez purchased this home in 1979. Desi Arnaz and Miguelito had a friendly feud over who sang Babalu better.

Ⓢ 1029 East El Alameda
DOROTHY LAMOUR

The sarong wearing femme fatale from the Road movies of Bing Crosby and Bob Hope lived in this 4 bed 3 bath 1,861sf home, built in 1935. On screen they were all romance and laughs, but in real life they seldom interracted. in 1931, at the age of 17, she was Miss New Orleans.

Ⓣ 1075 East El Alameda
GEORGE CHRISTY

Hollywood Reporter columnist and bit-part actor who was fired as a reporter for taking parts in films in exchange for good reviews lived here in 1974. The home was built in 1933 with 3 bedrooms and 3 baths in 2,353sf of living space on a 10,019sf lot with a pool.

Ⓤ 1165 East El Alameda

DICK WHITTINGHILL

In 1968, Pied Pipers band singer and KMPC AM radio disc jockey lived in this 1,916sf 2 bed 3 bath home which was built in 1936 on a 7,841sf lot. Dick was with KMPC for thirty years from 1950-1970.

Ⓥ 1188 East El Alameda

BOB & DOLORES HOPE

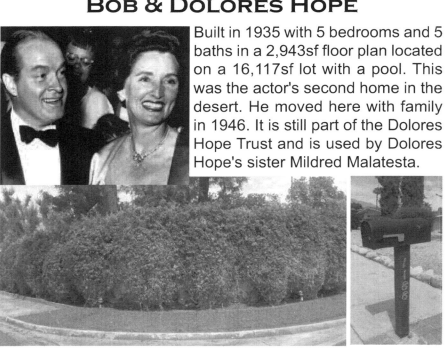

Built in 1935 with 5 bedrooms and 5 baths in a 2,943sf floor plan located on a 16,117sf lot with a pool. This was the actor's second home in the desert. He moved here with family in 1946. It is still part of the Dolores Hope Trust and is used by Dolores Hope's sister Mildred Malatesta.

Ⓦ **1232 East El Alameda**

HEDY LAMARR

Rumors that this was Austrian-born actress Hedy Lamarr's house could not be verified.

Ⓧ **1385 East El Alameda**

FRANCIS LEDERER

Fifty year actor of silent films, Broadway and TV's *Mission: Impossible* owned this 3 bed 2 bath home for nearly thrirty years till his death in 2000. After which it remained in the Marion Lederer Trust until it was sold in June of 2011. The home has 1,981sf on a 12,632sf lot and was built in 1953.

635 East Granvia Valmonte

DICK HAYMES

Actor and singer who sang Irish Eyes Are Smiling and It Might As Well Be Spring lived here in 1952. The 4 bed 5 bath 3,837sf home was built in 1936 on a 31,799sf lot.

GLORIA SWANSON

Actress best known for her portrayal of a faded silent film star in *Sunset Boulevard* (1950) turned sculptor turned health food guru owned the home from 1970-1975.

 ## 735 East Granvia Valmonte

MARION HUNTINGTON

Daughter of Southern Pacific Railroad Tycoon Henry Huntington, who owned this home and often referred to it as "The Huntington Estate." The home itself is an 11 bedroom and 10 bath 7,049sf main house, built in 1933 with a pool house and several other structures, including: a swimming pool and a tennis court, all on a 93,654sf lot. That's over two acres!

AC ## 1069 East Marshall Way

KIRK DOUGLAS

The original *Spartacus*, Doc Holliday in *Gunfight at the O.K. Corral* and Vincent Van Gogh in *Lust For Life's* first desert home, known as "Tachevah Vista." He lived in this home when it was new in 1955 for two years before moving to the Las Palmas neighborhood. The 2,095sf home has 4 bedrooms 3 baths and sits on a 11,326sf lot with a pool. Douglas starred in over 80 films, was nominated for 5 Academy Awards and authored 10 books including his autobiography The Ragman's Son, a New York Times best seller.

AD ## 291 East Mel Avenue

HERBERT ANDERSON

Actor who played *Dennis the Menace's* father on TV in 1960's lived here in the Rancho El Mirador condos in 1994.

AE 1540 East Mel Avenue
LES BAXTER

Composer, conductor of the 1950's Beach Parties films lived in this 3 bed 2 bath 2,046sf home on a 10,454sf lot. Baxter's career spanned everything from Nat King Cole albums to Sea World theme music. He was once heralded as writing the entire score to a movie in only 3 hours for $5000. His greatest contribution is the creation of exotic space music with his album Music Out of the Moon.

AF 550 East Miraleste Court
MAURICE ENOS

Director Busby Berkeley's brother lived in this 2 bed 2 bath 1,455sf home in 1974 until his death in 1993. The house was built in 1970 on a 20,338sf lot.

(AH) 720 East Paseo El Mirador
EDDIE CANTOR

Stage and film star lived here from 1944-1964 with his wife Ida in this 3 bed 3 bath 1,618sf 1941 home on a 16,117sf lot. Cantor was wiped out financially in the stock market crash of 1929 but his upbeat songs are credited with lifting America's spirits.

(AI) 730 East Paseo El Mirador
LAWRENCE WELK

Big band leader and variety television show producer owned this 2,749sf 3 bed 3 bath 1952 home till 1978. It has a pool and a 16,117sf lot. Welk was the creator of ballroom Champagne Music and was known for his corny German accent phrases like "Wunnerful, Wunnerful," "Ah-one and a-two" and "Pee (be) on your toes."

AJ ## 853 East Paseo El Mirador

TRUMAN CAPOTE

Southern gothic writer first rented and then bought this home in 1968. It was built in 1955, has 5 bedrooms and 4 baths, with 3,825sf of interior space and sits on a 14,810sf lot with a pool. While in the desert Capote paraded a bevy of beefcake male lovers to parties hosted by other celebs.

AK ## 1055 East Paseo El Mirador

KEELY SMITH

Las Vegas Singer & entertainer has lived in this home since 2006. Built in 1956, it's a 3 bed 2 bath with 1,786sf of living space and a pool on a 13,504sf lot. When Smith married Bobby Milano in 1975, Frank Sinatra gave away the bride. In February 2008, she performed with Kid Rock at the 50th Grammy Awards.

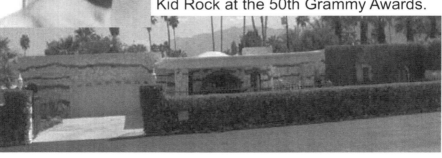

AL ## 630 East Tachevah Road
CHARLIE FARRELL

Last Palm Springs home of actor, Palm Springs celebrity pioneer, owner of The Racquet Club, and Mayor (1953-1970), Charlie Farrell, called Mr. Palm Springs, lived here for the last ten years of his life till he died on May 6th, 1990. The home was built in 1933 with 4 bedrooms 4 baths, 3,652sf and a pool on a 30,492sf lot.

AN ## 1145 East San Jacinto Way
BETTY GRABLE

Rumored to be the famed actress's home during her second marriage to Trumpetist Harry James, 1943-1965. Facts are uncertain as to the authenticity of this claim. The 3 bed 2 bath home was built in 1934 with 2,010sf of space on an 8,276sf lot.

AO **1575 East San Jacinto Way**

HARRY BRAND

20th Century Fox Director of Publicity purchased this home in 1956. It was built a year earlier in 1955 with 2 bedrooms 3 baths, 1,674sf of space & a pool on a 8,276sf lot.

RICHARD LANG

TV Director and son of Walter Lang, Director of *The King and* I and many other 20th Century Fox Musicals, purchased this home in 1974.

AP **650 East Tachevah Road**

WILLIAM MCCLATCHEY

Grandson of Sacramento Bee founder James McClatchy owned this 9 bed 12 bath home from 1995-2003. It has 7,823sf and a pool on a 34,848sf lot and was originally built in 1966.

(AQ) 1265 East Tachevah Road
MIGUELITO VALDEZ

In 1968, one of the five original Mambo Kings and original singer of Babalu - he was often called Mr. Babalu, much to Desi Arnaz's chagrin - lived in this 3 bed 3 bath 1,950sf home on a 5,663sf lot..

(AR) 1431 East Tachevah Road
EDMUND GOULDING

British director of Ginger Rogers in *Teenage Rebel*, Greta Garbo and John Barrymore in *Grand Hotel*, Tyrone Powers in *The Razor's Edge*, lived here in 1959, one year before he died. The 2 bed 2 bath 1,300sf home was built in 1956.

AS **1188 East Tamarisk Road**

NORMAN TAUROG

Academy Award winning director for *Boys Town* starring Mickey Rooney, who while at MGM and then at Paramount directed five Martin and Lewis comedies before making the desert classic *Palm Springs Weekend* with Robert Conrad, Troy Donahue and Connie Stevens, lived in this home in 1953.

AT **333 East Tamarisk Road**

RORY CALHOUN

Western actor and author who as a youth stole a gun and was sent to reform school and then broke out to go on a crime spree only to be recaptured and sent to San Quentin, moved here in 1970. This modest 2 bed 2 bath home has 1,124sf and was built in 1933.

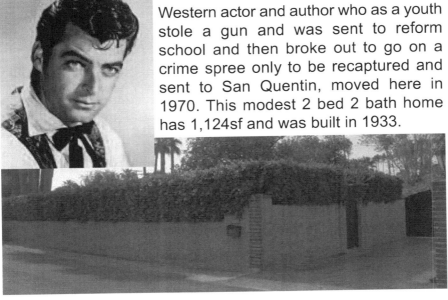

(AU) ## 346 East Tamarisk Road
JOSEPH SCHENCK

In 1893, at 15, Joseph schenck immigrated to the U.S. By 1909 he and his brother purchased the Palisades Amusement Park in New Jersey and then partnered with Marcus Loew to operate a chain of east coast movie theatres. He married film star Norma Talmadge in 1916 and then later moved to the west coast where movie history was being made. By 1933 he was President of United Artists. Schenck built this home in 1935 after divorcing Talmadge, the same year he partnered with Darryl Zanuck to found 20th Century Pictures and only two years before he merged it with William Fox's studio. The new company was named 20th Century Fox. In 1943 Schenck was found guilty of tax evasion coupled with a mob payola scandal to quiet unions.

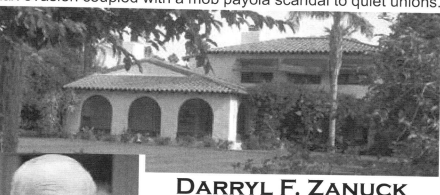

DARRYL F. ZANUCK

Quit as Head of Production at Warner Studios to found 20th Century Pictures with Joseph Schenck and became one of the creators of the movie studio system. His films include: *Grapes of Wrath, The Snake Pit*, and more. Zanuck conveniently won this house in a poker game from Schenck, who was trying to evade an IRS audit at the time. The home is 7,247sf with 10 bedrooms and 9 bathrooms on a 63,162sf lot. In 1979, Zanuck had a heart attack in this home which resulted with his death in Desert Hospital.

1129 East Tamarisk Road

WILLIAM GOETZ

In 1955, the Head of Production at 20th Century Fox and Universal, Louis B. Mayer's son-in-law. Goetz leased this 5 bed 6 bath 4,074sf home, built in 1938.

CAROL HEISS

In 1963, the Ice Capades Corp owned this home and five-time world champion ice skater Heiss lived here after making *Snow White and the Three Stooges.*

 1280 East Tamarisk Road

WINSTON HIBLER

Narrator and director of Disney nature films lived in this 4 bedroom 2 bath 1957 home with about 2,000sf on a 13,068sf lot.

AX 444 East Valmonte Norte
MICHAEL MASSER

Motown composer owned this 6 bed 3 bath 3,424sf home from 1991-99. It was built in 1937 on a 12,197sf lot. Masser has written hit songs for Whitney Houston, Gladys Knight, George Benson, and more. Masser and his wife Ogniana live in Palm Desert.

AY 487 East Valmonte Norte
MILTON SPERLING

Writer, producer who was Oscar nominated for the script *The Court Marshall of Billy Mitchell* lived here in 1956. The owner of Lyon's English Grille, David Lyons is the current owner. The home was built in 1937 with 3 bedrooms and 5 baths in 2,925sf of living space on a 13,504sf lot.

AZ 355 East Valmonte Sur

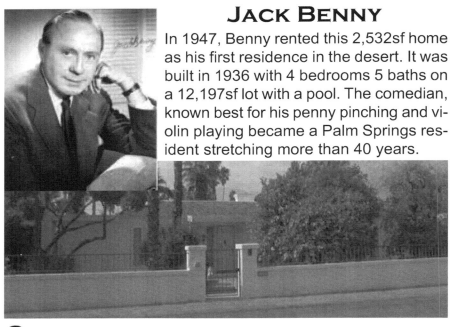

JACK BENNY

In 1947, Benny rented this 2,532sf home as his first residence in the desert. It was built in 1936 with 4 bedrooms 5 baths on a 12,197sf lot with a pool. The comedian, known best for his penny pinching and violin playing became a Palm Springs resident stretching more than 40 years.

BA 419 East Valmonte Sur

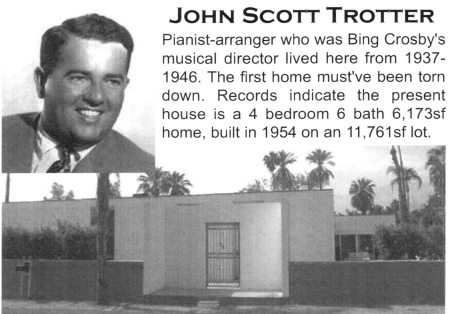

JOHN SCOTT TROTTER

Pianist-arranger who was Bing Crosby's musical director lived here from 1937-1946. The first home must've been torn down. Records indicate the present house is a 4 bedroom 6 bath 6,173sf home, built in 1954 on an 11,761sf lot.

BB 1285 East Verbena Drive

CARMEN MIRANDA

Miranda's first home in the desert before moving into her Deep Well abode. The Brazilian actress died in 1955 from a heart attack induced by a cocaine overdose. The 1943 house is 2 bed 2 bath, 1,128sf on a 12,632sf lot, with a pool.

BC 688 East Vereda Sur

IRVING FLORSHEIM

Shoemaker king owned this home in 1957. Built in 1950 it has 5 bedrooms 6 baths in 4,097sf of interior space and a pool on a very large 38,768sf lot.

JIM & TAMMY FAYE BAKKER

Televangelists hid out in this rented home in 1987 as their religious empire was crumbling and throngs of television news crews waited outside.

BD 723 East Vereda Sur/ 700 East Vereda Sur
IRVING BEECHER

Screenwriter of *Meet Me in St. Louis, The Life of Riley, Bye Bye Birdie*, and more, lived here from 1959-1979. Home now renumbered 700 Vereda Sur. The 3 bed 4 bath 3,568sf home was built in 1957 on a 27,878sf lot with a pool.

NOAH DIETRICH

Friend and financial advisor to Howard Hughes, bought this home in 1976. Shown here, Hughes is on the left, Dietrich on the right. Noah was fired in 1957.

BE 358 East Via Altamira
WILLIAM "BUSTER" COLLIER, JR.

Actor and husband to *Ziegfeld Follies* performer, Marie Stevens lived here in 1934. The home has 5 bedrooms & 5 baths with 3,799sf.

MARILYN MONROE

Claimed to be the home of Marilyn, although no evidence is known to support this. She was photo'd in PS in 1956.

BF ## 318 East Altamira

BUSBY BERKELEY

In 1958, the director of spectacular dance and water ballet musicals, whose real name was William Enos, moved into this 4 bed 3 bath 2,678sf Colonial home with a pool, where he lived until his death in Palm Springs on March 14, 1976. He is buried in Desert Memorial Park in Cathedral City.

BG ## 437 East Via Colusa

RONNIE ROBERTSON

1956 Olympic silver medalist best known for his spinning ability lived here in 1972, after his Ice Capades career. During his time in Palm Springs, he commuted to Hong Kong where he guest coached at City Plaza Ice Palace. The 1937 home has 3 bedrooms and 3 baths, 2,493sf and a pool on a 14,375sf lot.

BH 475 East Valmonte Sur

JOAN PERRY

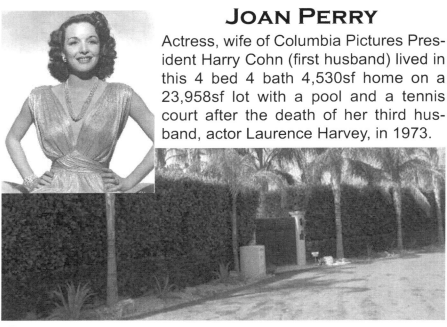

Actress, wife of Columbia Pictures President Harry Cohn (first husband) lived in this 4 bed 4 bath 4,530sf home on a 23,958sf lot with a pool and a tennis court after the death of her third husband, actor Laurence Harvey, in 1973.

BI 1120 Linda Vista Road

TEDDY HART

Played the indian "Crowbar" in the *Ma and Pa Kettle* movies lived here from 1968-1971. The 1951 home has 3 bedrooms and 3 baths in 1,812sf of living space on a 10,019sf lot.

BJ 888 North Avenida De Las Palmas

WILLIAM PEARLBERG

Paramount Pictures producer second Palm Springs home. Built in 1951 and designed by William F. Cody, the home has 4 bedrooms 4 baths, 2,716sf and a pool on a 15,682sf lot.

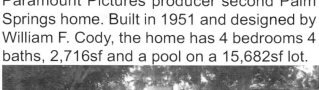

BL 928 North Avenida De Las Palmas

CARY GRANT

Grant and third wife, actress Betsy Drake, bought this home dubbed "Las Palomas" in 1954. It was built in 1927 with 4 bed 7 baths, 3,886sf on a 67,084sf lot and is a replica of an Andalusian farmhouse. Here he studied psychiatry, enjoyed bisexuality and dropped acid. He was listed in the local public phone book under his real name of Archibald Leach. He divorced Drake and remarried Dyan Cannon while living here. He sold it in 1972.

FRANK ZANE

Three time Mr. Olympia, 1977-79, bought this home of Cary Grant's and lived here from 1988-1998. Zane claimed to find scrapbooks and other forgotten memorabilia stored in the attic.

982 North Avenida De Las Palmas

JOHN PHILLIPS

This was the first desert home of Mamas and Papas singer in the desert, which Phillips rented in 1994 with musician, songwriter Scott McKenzie.

 **899 North Avenida De Las Palmas**

HAROLD LLOYD

This 7,006sf 5 bedroom 6 bath home was built by silent screen star Lloyd in 1925 on a 43,996sf lot with a pool. The actor owned it till his death in 1971. The rear entrance address is 878 Avenida Palos Verdes.

AL ADAMSON

In 1975, Adamson rented this palatial home to make the sexploitation movie *Blazing Stewardesses* starring Yvonne De Carlo. In 1995 Adamson was found murdered, his body stuffed under his hot tub.

172

BO 770 North Avenida Palos Verdes
DALE WASSERMAN

Playwright of *One Flew Over the Cuckoo's Nest* and *Man of La Mancha* lived here when the home was brand new. The 3 bed 4 bath home was built in 1974 with 4,156sf of interior space and a 19,166sf lot.

BP 877 North Avenida Palos Verdes
GEORGE MONTGOMERY
& DINAH SHORE

Built in 1952 with 3 bed 2 baths, 2,710sf on a 15,682sf lot with a pool, by the tall leading man. Montgomery had been married to Dinah Shore since 1943. He constructed a total of 11 homes for family and friends. They lived here until their divorce in 1962.

LINDA CHRISTIANSEN

Ladies Professional Golf Association member purchased the home in 1995.

BQ 987 North Avenida Palos Verdes

WILLIAM PEARLBERG

Paramount Pictures producer built this 3,336sf 5 bed 5 bath home in 1947. He then sold it to Jack Benny in 1951 and moved over to 888 North Avenida De Las Palmas. It sits on a 15,682sf lot with a pool..

JACK BENNY

In 1951, this became comedian & actor Benny's first owned desert home after purchasing it from the producer of two of his movies, Pearlberg. It was during these years that Benny broadcast *The Jack Benny Show* from The Plaza Theatre.

GEORGE BURNS & GRACIE ALLEN

Unconfirmed reports claim Benny's home to have been owned by the comedic acting duo.

BR 641 North Camino Real

TONY CURTIS & JANET LEIGH

The famous Hollywood couple bought this 4 bed 4 bath home, named "Camp Curtis," brand new in 1960 for $46,000. It has 3,204sf of space and a pool on a 13,504sf lot.They are shown here with daughters Kelly and Jamie Lee who shared the home with Curtis & Leigh until their divorce in 1962. Leigh sold it 2 years later.

BS 690 North Camino Real

DONALD WOODS

King of the B's and desert real estate agent, in 1988, retired to this 3 bed 4 bath 1,816sf home, built in 1960 on a 12,197sf lot. Though Woods mostly acted in second rate films such as *The Case of The Curious Bride*(1936), he did on occasion score a major title like *Watch on the Rhine*(1943).

175

BT 1600 Chia Road East/1445 North Sunrise Way
HOWARD HUGHES

America's first billionaire owned a home here when this was called The Ranch Club, a premier Dude Ranch. This home has since been torn down and replaced by condominiums called The Ranch and the address has been changed to 1445 Sunrise Canyon Way.

BV 1550 North Indian Canyon Drive
ERROL FLYNN

Renumbered 1553 Chaparral Road and now called Desert Shadows Inn - a clothing optional resort complete with a Nudist Bridge. At one time this site was occupied by Casa Del Sol, which was again later renamed Normandy Inn, the original clothing optional hotel owned by Errol Flynn in 1943 after he was acquitted on charges of statutory rape.

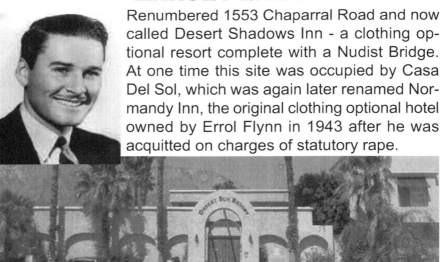

BX **570 North Via Corta** (continued on next page...)

CHARLES CORRELL

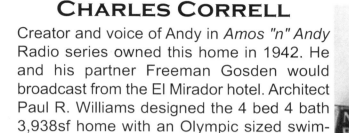

Creator and voice of Andy in *Amos "n" Andy* Radio series owned this home in 1942. He and his partner Freeman Gosden would broadcast from the El Mirador hotel. Architect Paul R. Williams designed the 4 bed 4 bath 3,938sf home with an Olympic sized swimming pool and a gazebo on a 57,499sf lot.

CHI - CHI

DINNER

ENTERTAINMENT

Call P Spgs 7391

217 N. Palm Canyon Dr. Palm Springs

From the 1949 Palm Springs Phone Directory.

570 North Via Corta (continued...)

JAY PALEY

Uncle and financial backer to President of CBS William Paley, Jay bought this home & sold it to Al Jolson

AL JOLSON

Purchased this home in 1946 from Jay Paley. The sale of this home to Jolson is believed to have been an inducement for Jolson to leave ABC and come to work for CBS.

NORMAN KRASNA

After Jolson's death in 1950, Broadway playwright and director Krasna married Jolson's widow, Erle Galbraith, and was the owner of the home till 1955.

FRANK SINATRA

Sinatra stayed here between takes from the making of *Pal Joey* during the brief interlude of selling his Palm Springs home and while waiting for his Tamarisk Country Club home to be finished in 1957.

DONALD DUNCAN

Duncan Toys mogul owned this home in 1960.

ALLAN JONES

Evangelical singer turned Hollywood performer, Allan Jones owned this home in 1965. His earliest role was in a Marx Brothers movie, yet his best role was as Gaylord Ravenal in *Showboat*. His son is musician Jack Jones.

KENNETH ANGER

Author of Hollywood Babylon, Scorpio Rising lived in the guest house here in 1995 and claimed the home was haunted by the ghost of Al Jolson. Anger is also a short film producer.

BY **796 North Via Miraleste**

HARRY HANBURY

Oklahoma self-made millionaire and Congressman, Hanbury built this Spanish Colonial estate in 1934. This home boasts 8 bedrooms and 8 bathrooms, has 5,370sf of interior space, a guest house, and a pool on a 85,813sf lot. It was designed by architect Ross Montgomery. Home has often been wrongly acclaimed to be the home of Howard Hughes or Barbara or Betty Hutton because of the H H monogrammed gate posts.

CARY GRANT & BARBARA HUTTON

Grant and new bride, Woolworth heiress, Barbara Hutton honeymooned here in 1948.

DAVID O. SELZNICK

Gone With the Wind, King Kong, A Farewell to Arms, A Tale of Two Cities and more, producer Selznick rented this home in 1954. During his thirty year career, Selznick produced 87 movies, directed three and wrote ten.

PHIL REGAN

Singing New York Cop turned actor's second home in the desert. He owned it from the late 1960's to the mid 1970's. Regan became an actor after guarding a Vaudeville party let him show his talents. In 2001 it qualified for a $1mil mortgage.

BZ 650 North Via Miraleste
EDWIN H. MORRIS

First Palm Springs home of the world's largest music publisher. It was built in 1939, has 6 bedrooms 7 baths, 6,456sf and a pool on a 75,794sf lot.

CA 1194 North Via Miraleste
LUCILLE BALL & DESI ARNAZ

It's claimed the famous couple rented this beautiful 6 bed 6 bath 2,801sf home, built in 1936 on a 16,117sf lot with a pool, as their marriage and careers grew and they sought more privacy, though still wanted to be a part of the El Mirador crowd. Yet, when I contacted Lucie Arnaz aout this, she directed a staff member to me to say, "They never lived there."

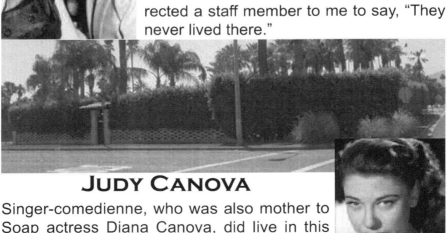

JUDY CANOVA

Singer-comedienne, who was also mother to Soap actress Diana Canova, did live in this beautiful home from 1956-1959.

1185 Pasatiempo Road East

HOWARD HUGHES

America's first billionaire, in 1963, owned this 1955 home with 3 bedrooms and 2 baths in 1,631sf on a 11,326sf lot, while purchasing Las Vegas casinos: Desert Inn, Frontier, Sands and Silver Slipper.

1220 Pasatiempo Road East

NICK CASTLE

Built in 1956 on a 10,019sf lot, with 3 bedrooms and 2 baths in 1,966sf, this was the former home of dance director to many celebrities, including Shirley Temple, Fred Astaire, and more.

CD 1225 Pasatiempo Road East
NORMAN TOKAR

Director of 93 episodes of *Leave It To Beaver*, Walt Disney movies *The Apple Dumpling Gang* starring Don Knotts, Bill-Bixby and Tim Conway, lived in this 3 bed 2 bath 1,864sf home with a pool on a 10,019sf lot, built in 1955.

CE 1240 Pasatiempo Road East
CAMERON CROWE

Writer, director of *Jerry Maguire, Almost Famous*, and more, who at only 18 was a reporter for Rolling Stone magazine, lived here with his realtor-father, James Crowe, in this 3 bedroom 2 bath, 1420sf home, until the family moved to Indio in 1973. In 1979, Crowe went back to high school, in San Diego, to research his book *Fast Times at Ridgemont High*, a best seller and a movie.

CF **1265 Serena Circle**

EDEN HARTFORD

Actress and third wife of Groucho Marx owned this 3 bed 2 bath home when it was brand new from 1980-1983. It's 1,716sf on a 12,197sf lot with a pool.

CG **1400 East Tamarisk Road**

JOAN DAVIS

In 1961, radio: *The Rudy Valle Show*, actress: Roy Rogers and Abbot & Costello movies, died of a heart attack while living in this home, which was built in 1949 with 2 bed 2 baths, 1,470sf on a 10,454sf lot.

CH 1036 East Via Altamira

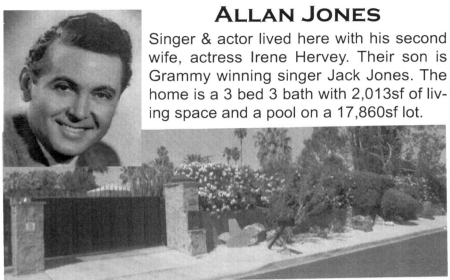

ALLAN JONES

Singer & actor lived here with his second wife, actress Irene Hervey. Their son is Grammy winning singer Jack Jones. The home is a 3 bed 3 bath with 2,013sf of living space and a pool on a 17,860sf lot.

CI 1049 East Via Altamira

VAN JOHNSON

Actor of *5 Seconds Over Tokyo* and *The Caine Mutiny* and his wife Eve Abbot bought this home in 1955. The couple lived here with custody of best friend, Keenan Wynn's, two sons (Ned and Tracy), who was a frequent visitor. It's often been speculated this atypical threesome was hiding a homosexual lifestyle for Johnson.

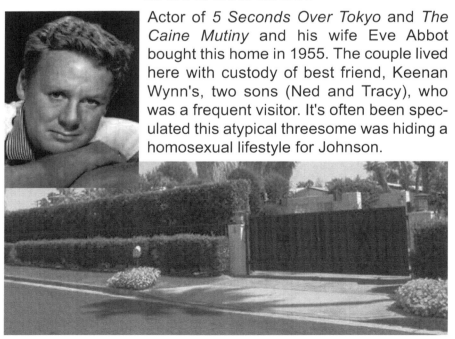

ⓒⱼ 1066 East Via Altamira

GREGORY GAYE

In 1975, this 50 year veteran actor (1928-79) known for playing German Generals and Russian royalty owned this 3 bed 4 bath 3,127sf home, built in 1947.

ⒸⓁ 572 North Indian Canyon Drive

JACK DEMPSEY

Heavyweight boxer and his fourth wife (1958), Deanna Paitelli, maintained a suite at the Howard Manor, now known as the Colony Palms Hotel.

HOWARD MANOR

Built in 1936, by Chicago Purple Gang member Al Wertheimer, the red roofed expansive hotel was originally called the Colonial House and hosted an illegal gambling hall in the basement. In 1951 L.A. millionaires Bob Howard & Andrea Leeds hired architect Stewart Williams and designer O.E.L. Graves to remodel the property, which from then on was called the Howard Manor.

CM 640 North Indian Canyon Drive

SPANISH INN

in 1972, the hotel was bought by actor Alan Ladd's (*Shane,* 1953) widow, actress Sue Carroll. She and her husband had been long-time Palm Springs residents and also owned Ladd's Hardware store.

CN 1276 North Indian Canyon Drive

LONE PALM HOTEL

Lone Palm Hotel owned by Musical Knights bandleader, Horace Heidt. His shows were heard on both NBC and CBS from 1932-53. The hotel is no longer standing.

FRANK SINATRA

This was the first place Sinatra stayed when coming to the desert in 1944 with his first wife, Nancy Barbato.

HOWARD MANOR
FABULOUS FOOD
BEVERAGES
Poolside or in The MANOR ROOM
Magnificient Accommodations
Visitors and Villagers Welcome
572 N. Indian Ave.   Phone 2227
ROBERT S. HOWARD, Host

Howard Manor
1954 Palm Springs
Phone Directory
Advertisement

Lone Palm Hotel 1957
Palm Springs Phone
Directory Advertisement

Two Big Swimming Pools,
Wading Pool for Children,
Colorful Caravan Dining Room,
Cocktail Lounge,
Television Room,
Attractive Accommodations.

1276 N. Indian Avenue

CALL

FAirview

4-1411

HORACE HEIDT'S

Lone Palm Hotel

PALM SPRINGS, CALIFORNIA

Your Hosts - Jack & Jerry Heidt

187

Eric G. Meeks Collection

The intersection of Sunrise Way and Vista Chino Drive, at about 6:30am, is one of the best locations to view the shadow of the Witch of Tahquitz in Tahquitz Canyon.

Central Palm Springs
Sunrise and Airport Neighborhoods

Back in the day, this was considered the boonies. The homes are sparse and the land unevenly settled. The men who lay claim to fame in this neighborhood were of the rough and tumble variety, one was a child star, another a clown.

A few of the homes go back to post World War II, most were built in the 1960's and later. The land was developed later in Palm Springs history because it is moslty Cahuilla Indian lease land and until the 1960's, when Judge McCabe cleared legislation to make the land bondable, banks would not lend on the properties.

But once new laws were passed, the same developers came into this area and built the post and beam mid-century affordable houses that have become the mainstay of the Little City of Big Screen Stars.

You'll find condo associations like Desert Lanai, Sagewood, Sunrise Oasis, Sunrise Racquet Club, and single family homes like Sun Villas. All of moderate square footage, 1,200-2,000sf, and sporting a variety of designs.

The celebrities are fewer here and mostly of later generations. But they each have their own history and are still worthy of note. After all, the A-list wouldn't be the top if there weren't others to lay the supporting foundation beneath them.

Central Palm Springs: Sunrise and Airport Neighborhoods

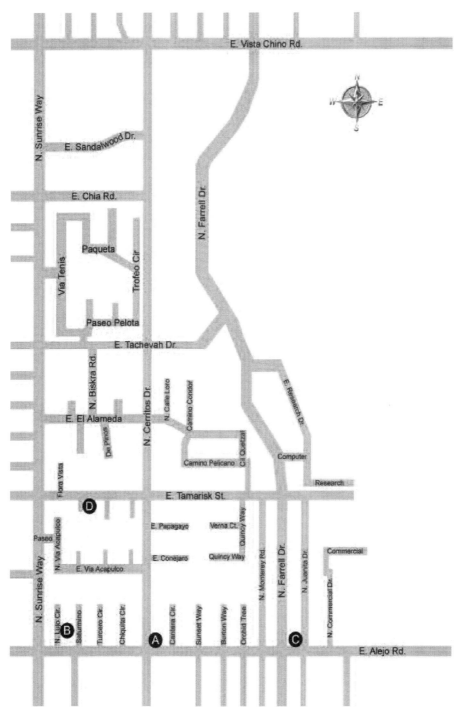

(A) 502 North Cerritos Drive

CHRIS ALCAIDE

Until his death in 2004, cowboy detective story arch-villain actor, Alcaide, lived in this 2,895sf 4 bed 3 bath home, built in 1977, with his photographer wife Peri Hatman. Alcaide played in 118 TV and movie titles between 1950 and 1987, including *The Big Valley, The Fugitive*, and *Perry Mason*.

(B) 501 North Juanita Road

STEPHEN BOYD

Actor who fought against Charlton Heston in the chariot race scene in *Ben-Hur* and then became typecast for other 1960's historical epics, lived in this 2 bedroom 2 bath 1,360sf home in 1965. It was built in 1960 on a 12,197sf lot.

Ⓒ 540 North Lujo Circle

BOB ANDERSON

Actor who started by paying a hungry boy in *Grapes of Wrath*(1940) and later played Little George in *It's a Wonderful Life* before becoming a sound mixer and then production manager: *Passenger 57, Demolition Man*, lives in this 3 bed 2 bath 1,541sf home, built in 1973 on a 11,326sf lot.

Ⓓ 792 North Madrid Circle

GIL LAMBERT

Vaudeville contortionist actor who later played Bozo the Clown lived in this 1972 home, owned by his wife Irene Griffith, in 1986. It's a 3 bed and 3 bath with 1,387sf.

Eric G. Meeks Collection

This photo of Frank Sinatra was taken during the 1960's in the Palm Springs area, although the exact location is unknown.

Tennis Club

Tennis Club

Palm Springs oldest neighborhood hosts an ancient Indian burial ground and the homes of Palm Springs earliest pioneers Judge John J. McCallum and Nellie Coffman. It hosts such important structures as a former Spanish estate - now the Ingleside Inn, the O'Donnell House(Class I historic Site), the Willows(Class I Historic site), Le Vallauris(Class I Historic Site), the Korakia Pensione, the Casa Cody(built by the cousin of Buffalo Bill Cody), the Desert Museum and the Palm Springs Tennis Club, built in 1937, and namesake to the neighborhood.

The area, bounded by Ramon Road to the South and Tahquitz Canyon Drive to the north (we'll enlarge the nighborhood by one block for this book), and byPalm Canyon Drive on the east and the rocky face of Mount San Jacinto on the west (again, let's stretch it one more block to Indian Canyon Drive for our purposes here).

Some of the adobe structures here go back to the late 1800's. The hotels began cropping up in the 1920's.

Due to the longevity of its largesse, it is the most eclectic of the neighborhoods. You'll see a Morrocan themed hotel, Spanish Revivalist architecture, Mid-Century Moderns, an East Coast Gingerbread, and California Ranch styled homes, buildings, and celebity businesses.

Keep your cameras ready. You'll want to use a whole roll of film here. You may even want to exit the car and visit some of the unique boutique hotels. Their storied lobbies and bouganvillea patios will enthrall you, while the streetside restaurants of downtown immerse you in the luxury of old Palm Springs.

195

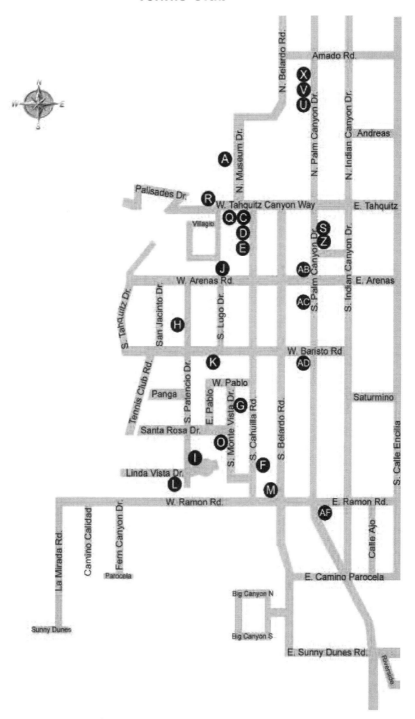

Ⓐ ## 101 Museum Drive

DESERT MUSEUM

Originally built in 1938 as a stuffed wildlife exhibit, the museum has undergone several expansions including the addition of the Annenberg Theater in 1976 and the Steve Chase Art Wing in 1995, which was designed by architect E. Stewart Williams.

Ⓒ ## 115 South Cahuilla Road

NELLIE COFFMAN

Palm Springs pioneers former home, now located at The Village Green, 221 South Palm Canyon Drive, and is the site of the Palm Springs Historical Society.

WILLIAM GARGAN

In 1958, the Ellery Queen actor, who played in films from 1928-1949 and then switched to TV for another decade, resided here at Nellie Coffman's former estate.

Ⓓ 161 South Cahuilla Road

POLLY BERGEN

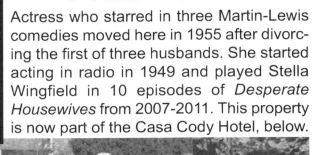

Actress who starred in three Martin-Lewis comedies moved here in 1955 after divorcing the first of three husbands. She started acting in radio in 1949 and played Stella Wingfield in 10 episodes of *Desperate Housewives* from 2007-2011. This property is now part of the Casa Cody Hotel, below.

Ⓔ 175 South Cahuilla Circle

HARRIET CODY

The Casa Cody was built in 1936 and was the city's first horse stables where Tom Mix and Jack Holt boarded horses. Harriet Cody was the widow of Harold Cody, first cousin to Wild West Showman Buffalo Bill.

F 430 South Cahuilla Road
COLONY BUNGALOWS

Hotel owned and operated by artist Earl Cordrey in 1944 who, besides great Americana artwork and desert scapes, also created the City of Palm Springs logo. The hotel is now called Michael's House.

G 372 South Monte Vista Drive
WILLIAM BENDIX

Actor who played in 88 titles from 1942-1965 resided here with his wife Theresa. Bendix was best known for playing Chester A. Riley in *Life of Riley*(1949) and portraying The Babe in *The Babe Ruth Story*(1948). The 3 bed 3 bath home was built in 1948 with 1,606sf and a pool on a 8,712sf lot.

Ⓗ 257 South Patencio Road
KORAKIA PENSIONE

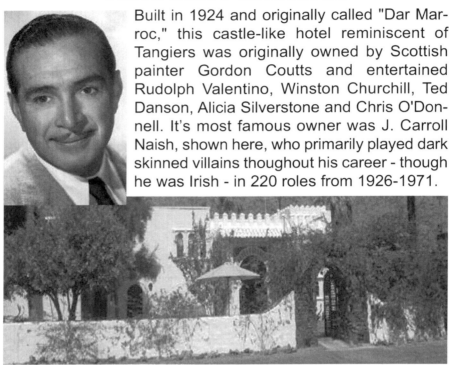

Built in 1924 and originally called "Dar Marroc," this castle-like hotel reminiscent of Tangiers was originally owned by Scottish painter Gordon Coutts and entertained Rudolph Valentino, Winston Churchill, Ted Danson, Alicia Silverstone and Chris O'Donnell. It's most famous owner was J. Carroll Naish, shown here, who primarily played dark skinned villains thoughout his career - though he was Irish - in 220 roles from 1926-1971.

Ⓘ 466 South Patencio Road
ARTHUR K. BOURNE

Billionaire playboy son who inherited a Singer Sewing Machine director's fortune had Walter Neff design and build this 3 bed 4 bath 3,077sf home on a 10,019sf lot in 1933.

J 370 West Arenas Road

JAMES WHALE

The Hideaway hotel was the former home of openly gay British born director of American Horror (*Frankenstein*, 1931) and later, theatrical musicals. Whale committed suicide in the pool in 1957. The hotel was designed by modernist architect Herbert Burns.

K 377 West Baristo Road

NANCY KULP

Beverly Hillbillies secretary and suspected lesbian died here of cancer while recuperating with her friend Joseph Baier in 1989. The 3 bed 4 bath 2,464sf home was built in 1976 on a 9,583sf lot.

ⓛ 511 West Linda Vista Drive

CHARLES IRWIN

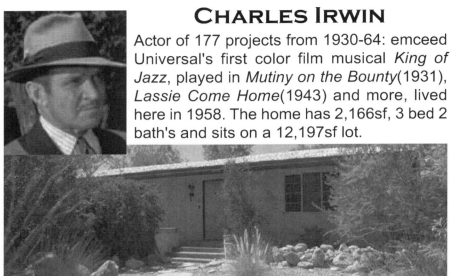

Actor of 177 projects from 1930-64: emceed Universal's first color film musical *King of Jazz*, played in *Mutiny on the Bounty*(1931), *Lassie Come Home*(1943) and more, lived here in 1958. The home has 2,166sf, 3 bed 2 bath's and sits on a 12,197sf lot.

Ⓜ 200 West Ramon Road

INGLESIDE INN

Melvyn Haber has owned this hotel since 1975 when he unknowingly kicked Steve McQueen and Ali McGraw off property because of their rough appearance on a motorcycle. Built in 1922 and originally called Twin Palms. Home and hotel to many celebrities over the years: Lily Pons, Howard Hughes, Ava Gardner, Salvador Dali, Bank of America founder A.P. Giannini, Lucille Ball. In 1976, it was the site of Frank and Barbara Sinatra's pre-wedding dinner. In the 1980's, Kurt Russell and Goldie Hawn were known to fly into town to have lunch here.

◎ 421 West Santa Rosa Drive

HERMAN RIDDER

Grandson of Knight-Ridder newspaper group's founder owned this home for more than 12 years. It was built in 1939 with 3 bedrooms 4 baths in 4,864sf of living space on a 27,007sf lot.

ⓠ 385 West Tahquitz Canyon Way

GEORGE ROBERSON

This Mediterranean/Spanish revival stone walled house was built in 1924 by Roberson, the son of Palm Springs pioneer Nellie Coffman. Currently the home is Le Vallauris Restaurant.

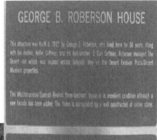

Ⓡ 412 Tahquitz Canyon Way

SAMUEL UNTERMEYER

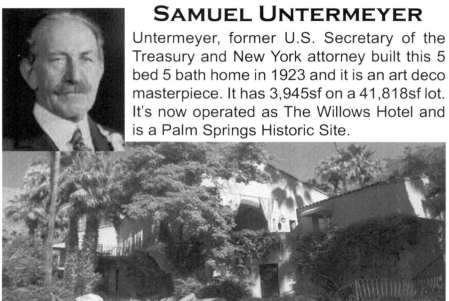

Untermeyer, former U.S. Secretary of the Treasury and New York attorney built this 5 bed 5 bath home in 1923 and it is an art deco masterpiece. It has 3,945sf on a 41,818sf lot. It's now operated as The Willows Hotel and is a Palm Springs Historic Site.

Ⓢ 100 Jack Benny Plaza/128 S. Palm Canyon Dr.

THE PLAZA THEATRE

Actual address is 128 South Palm Canyon Drive. Built in 1936 by Earl and Ethel Strebe when their movie nights at The Desert Inn grew too large, the historied theatre has broadcasted, movie premieres, *The Jack Benny Show* and *The Amos & Andy Show*. Currently it's the home of The Palm Springs Fabulous Follies and is owned by the Community Development Agency of the City of Palm Springs. Producer Riff Markowitz is the leaseholder.

Ⓤ 153 North Palm Canyon Drive

THE DESERT INN
& MARION DAVIES

The Desert Inn was originally built by Palm Springs settler Nellie Coffman who operated it for 40 years. Davies purchased the Desert Inn in 1955 for $1.75mil from Nellie's sons Earl Coffman and George Roberson. She sold it in 1960 for $2.5mil. The address is now the location of the Desert Fashion Plaza and the site of The three stories tall Marilyn Monroe statue, by

artist Seward Johnson (80 years old), who is also heir to the Johnson & Johnson fortune.

Below is a photo of the hotel during it's hey day, when guests were a parade of Hollywood stars and other prestigious persons who wanted to partake of the best of Palm Springs hospitality.

Ⓥ 217 North Palm Canyon Drive
CHI CHI CLUB & STARLITE ROOM

Owner Irwin Shuman's best known Palm Springs nightclub, built in 1931 when he converted The Waffle House, and where many celebrities both entertained and visited. The Chi Chi was here for some forty years before being torn down in 1977. In its hey day, it played host to Hollywood's elite and society's most prestigious personages. A few of the happenstances which occurred here included: Nat King Cole being ushered in through the back door in the days before blacks were accepted, Desi Arnazes Orchestra opened here in October 1950, and Frank Sinatra met Ava Gardner during a partner switch dance called by the Emcee during the early 1950's, while he was still married to Nancy Barbato. The ad to the right is from the 1963 PS phone directory.

1963 Palm Springs Phone Directory Advertisement

249 North Palm Canyon Drive

SY DEVORE MEN'S STORE

Clothing store owned by the Tailor to the Stars renowned for his design of Liberace's gold lame smoking jacket and Elvis Presley's rhinestone studded leather jumpsuits and capes for his second run in Las Vegas. Sy Devore also built a home in the Racquet Club Estates in 1959. The advertisement below is taken from the 1963 Palm Springs Phone directory. His store was about where the Hyatt Hotel is located downtown now.

Ⓩ 138 South Palm Canyon Drive
BERNARD OF HOLLYWOOD

Desert photography studio of Bruno Bernard, the famous Bernard of Hollywood. Bernard saw Palm Springs as an opportunity to further cement his name as Photographer to the Stars by keeping a studio open in Palm Springs. The location now is home to a Birkenstock shoe store. He also owned a home in the Las Palmas neighborhood until his death in 1991.

1944 Palm Springs Phone Directory Ad.

Bernard of Hollywood Studios

For portraiture which is glamourously different, our studios have set a new standard in high type photography

PALM SPRINGS
Plaza
Tel. 7151

HOLLYWOOD
9055 Sunset Blvd.

193 South Palm Canyon Drive

ANDREA LEEDS

Actress, 24 films between 1933-44, who owned the jewelry store Andrea of Palm Springs. She was also the wife of Bob Howard, son of the owner of the racehorse Seabiscuit, who went through millions of dollars of inheritance in a very short period of time. The 1944 Palm Springs phone directory shows Andrea with dual shops in The El Mirador & Howard Manor Hotels. The ad below is from the 1954 phone book. Location is now home to PS General Store. She also co-owned the Howard Manor.

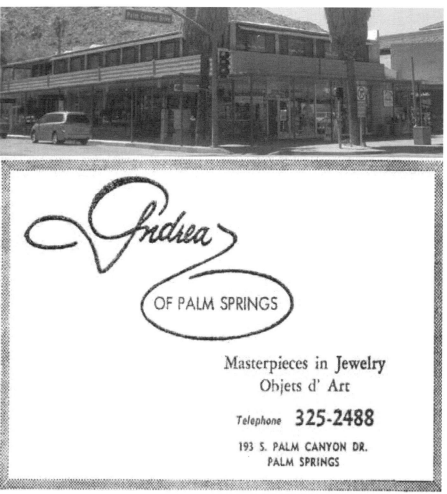

210

 219 South Palm Canyon Drive
JOLIE GABOR PEARL SALON

Pearl Salon Jewelry store owned by the mother of the Gabor sisters. The advertisement below is from the 1963 Palm Springs phone directory. The Palm Springs Heritage Center is now located where the Pearl Salon once stood. Jolie owned a home at the top of the Little Tuscany neighborhood. Her daughters Zsa Zsa, Eva and Magda were also PS residents.

Jolie Gabor Invites You to Her Fabulous

PEARL-JEWELRY
SALON
219 S. PALM CANYON DR.
32 4-2761

AD ## 333 South Palm Canyon Drive
ROBINSON'S SPECIALTY SHOP

Now the Alley, the Robinson's Specialty Shop was the only major retailer in Palm Springs for decades and therefore the number one place where celebrities and Palm Springs elite shopped. The building was designed by Hollywood production designer William L. Pereira and Charles Luckman.

Robinson's *Palm Springs*

A WORLD OF FASHION
FOR WOMEN, MEN
AND CHILDREN

GIFTS

SHOES

ACCESSORIES

★ ★ ★

PHONE: **32 4-9691**

333 SOUTH PALM CANYON DR.

From the 1963 Palm Springs Phone Directory.

AF 533 South Palm Canyon Drive
ALAN LADD'S HARDWARE

The Alan Ladd building was owned and operated by the famous actor and his wife Sue Carroll(acted in 26 titles from 1927-37), and sold hardware, retail and sporting goods beginning in 1955. Ladd is credited with 96 roles from 1932-64, including his most famous as the reluctant gunslinger in the western *Shane*(1953).

From the 1963 Palm Springs Phone Directory.

Alan
Ladd's
HARDWARE

* BUILDERS HARDWARE
* GENERAL HARDWARE
* APPLIANCES
* HOUSEWARES
* GIFTS
* PAINTS
* TOYS
* PATIO SUPPLIES

533 S. Palm Canyon Dr.

Dial 32 5-2165

213

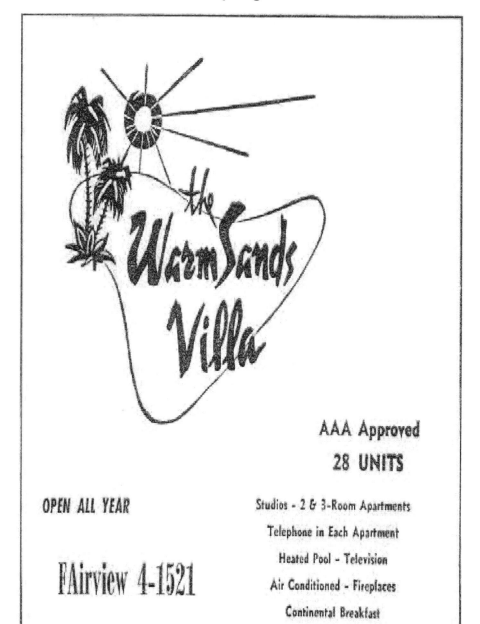

From the 1958 Palm Springs Phone directory.

Central Palm Springs
Warm Sands

Originally a small street of inexpensive boutique hotels running between Ramon Road and Sunny Dunes, this neighborhood has been revitalized in the past twenty years or so by a cadre of investors and visitors who have remodeled not only the hotels into trendy Gay, and sometimes clothing optional, hotspots, and like the hotel guests of The Racquet Club & El Mirador have seen the former guests become permanent homeowners, improving an entire neighborhood of mostly smallish run down fixer-uppers into a very stylish and desirous group of homes.

For these reasons, we'll respectively use the name Warm Sands to encompass a much larger section of Central Palm Springs, that's mostly undeveloped Indian Tribal land and has but a few districts of businesses, hotels, condos and homes. It began being developed in the 1920's with mostly smaller 1,000sf-ish homes although there are a few grand estates and the building continued at even pace through all the decades. Then in the 1970's a few developers saw the need to construct condominium associations and they were peppered in, and along Indian Canyon Drive there was a particular restaurant of reknowned flair we'll touch on at the end of the chapter.

Working class folks spawned working class celebrities, or at least a few who preferred to hide their talents amongst the middle class. Singers, writers, designers, actors & actresses and more hid out in the affordable area of Warm Sands and even one Angelic actress purchased her piece of Palm Springs on the rented slab of the Ramon (mobile home) Park. But does the cost of paradise matter? All want their moment in the sun.

Central Palm Springs: Warm Sands

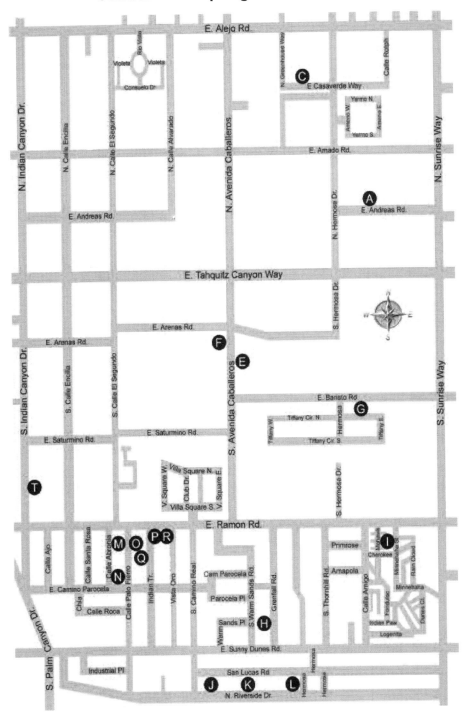

Ⓐ 1360 East Andreas Road
ROBERT RANDOLPH

Film and Broadway set designer owned a home here from 1994-1998. Randolph did the lighting and set design for the 1961 Broadway production of *How To Succeed in Business Without Really Trying* and the set design for the 1974 production of *Gypsy*. He died in March 2003 while still living in Palm Springs.

Ⓒ 1172 East Casa Verde Way
MARTIN RAGAWAY

Scriptwriter for *Abbot & Costello, Ma & Pa Kettle, Partridge Family, Brady Bunch,* more, lived in these condos till 1989. In retirement he wrote humorous golf books. The home was built in 1974, has 2 bedrooms and 2 baths with 1,221sf of living space.

Ⓔ 280 South Avenida Caballeros
ROY DEAN

Actor of 31 projects, mostly on Television, starting from 1947's *Hamlet*, where he played Lucianus, to *The Unexplained*(1991), who also pioneered male nude photography, bought a condo here in 1998. Caballeros Estates I are 1 and 2 bedroom condos. He died in Palm Springs in June of 2002.

Ⓕ 255 South Avenida Caballeros #106
MENAHEM GOLAN

Producer, director, writer, lives in Villa Caballeros Condominiums in a 2 bedroom 2 bath 1,046sf condo with 1,946sf with his wife Hedva. From 1964-2007 Golan produced more than 200 films in his career, including *Captain America* and *Night of the Living Dead* (both in 1990).

G 1369 South Tiffany Circle
LAURA LA PLANTE

Actress who started in Silent films and made the transition into talkies and beyond while mostly working with Universal, lived here in 1989 until her death in 1996, at the age of 94.

H 671 Grenfall Road
GITTA ALPAR

Pre-WWII German Film and Hungarian Opera star who came to America during the rise of the Nazi's. At one time she was married to *Metropolis* film leading man Gustav Froelich. She retired here in the 1960's and gave singing lessons. The home, dubbed "Villa DuBarry" was built in 1956 and consists of 2,904sf with 2 bedrooms and 3 bathrooms atop a sizable 13,504sf lot.

217 Minnehaha Street

DELLA REESE

Baptist minister and *Touched By An Angel* actress lived in a motor home at the Ramon (mobile home) Park. Reese began her acting career playing Rose on *The Mod Squad* (1968) and also did *Harlem Nights* with Eddie Murphy and Richard Pryor; *Beauty Shop* with Queen Latifah. She's been in 63 titles so far.

844 North Riverside Drive

BRAD DUNNING

Los Angeles Interior Designer with the foresight in 1996 to purchase this smallish 2 bedroom 2 bath 1,268sf home for $117,000 and begin the remodeling craze that has perpetuated a strong local real estate market. He sold it in 2002 for $305,000.

K 952 North Riverside Drive
LILA DAMITA

French actress, who played against Gary Cooper in *Fighting Caravans*(1931), was married to Errol Flynn from 1935-1942 and lived at this home in 1956. it was built in 1953, has 3 bedrooms and 2 baths, with 1,953sf of space on a 10,019sf lot.

L 1150 North Riverside Drive
AKIM TAMIROFF

60 year veteran actor twice nominated Best Supporting Actor lived here from 1960-1972, when he died of cancer. His widow lived here in this 4 bed 4bath 1952 home for another 11 years. Tamiroff played Sancho Panza in *Don Quixote*(1992), Anniello in *Hotel Paradiso*(1966), Spyros Acebos in *Ocean's Eleven*(1960), and many more.

Ⓜ 524 South Calle Abronia
HENRY WILCOXON

Played Marc Antony in Demille's *Cleopatra* (1934), and the Bishop in *Caddyshack* (1980), associate producer of *Samson and Delilah*(1949) and *The Ten Commandments* (1956). He acted in 71 titles between 1931 and 1983. Wilcoxon lived here in 1959.

Ⓝ 594 South Calle Abronia
RUSSELL WADE

RKO actor and real estate developer was the first owner of this home, built in 1948. It has 4 bedrooms and 4 baths with 1,936sf of living space on a 6,098sf lot. Wade is best known for his Westerns, Sci-Fi and Horror film work in the 1930's-40;s: *The Body Snatchers, The Ghost Ship,* & more.

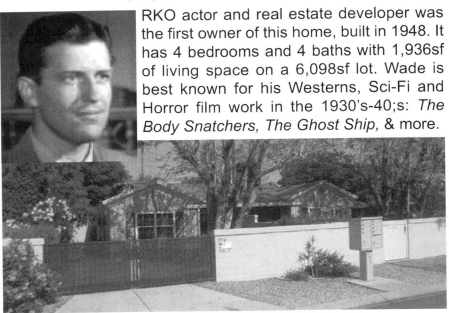

◉ 526 South Calle Palo Fiero

PAUL GRIMM

Artist who painted desert landscapes, Mount San Jacinto and the Sierra Nevada range lived here till he died in 1974. The small, 1,031sf, home was built in 1935 with 2 bedrooms and 2 baths. It sits on a 6,098sf lot. These days it has a pool.

℗ 504 South Indian Trail

LESLIE CHARTERIS

Mystery author who, in 1939, wrote The Saint in Palm Springs while staying here. The stucco and tile 2,660sf home was designed by architect Walter Neff and built in 1935. It has 4 bedrooms and 3 bathrooms atop a massive 21,780sf corner lot.

Ⓠ 527 South Indian Trail

JOHN M. STAHL

Producer of 66 titles, director of 46 titles, lived here in 1946. The 2 bed 2 bath 1,857sf home was built in 1936 on a 6,098sf lot. Stahl began his career directing *A Boy and the Law* in 1914. Other works include: *The Cavelier*(1928), *Magnificent Obsession* (1935), & *The Keys of the Kingdom*(1944).

Ⓡ 539 Vista Oro

BILL HAY

Pepsodent Toothpaste Radio announcer for *Amos "n" Andy* bought this 4 bed 4 bath 2,289sf 1937 home in 1938. It sits on a 12,197sf lot with a pool. *Amos "n" Andy* was the first syndicated radio show and it's sponsor Pepsodent contractually stipulated that no one but Hay would be its announcer.

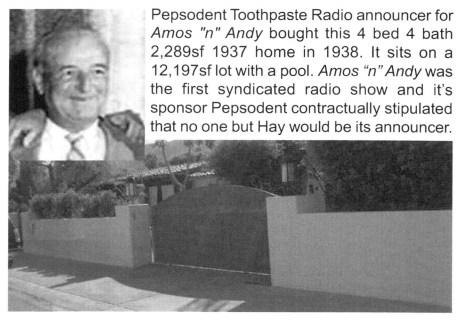

T ## 424 South Indian Canyon Drive
JILLY RIZZO

Jilly's was a restaurant & Bar owned by one of Sinatra's closest friends and host to many celebrity patrons. Jilly was mentioned in several Sinatra songs, had a part in the movie *The Manchurian Candidate* and often had one-liners on *Rowan and Martin's Laugh-In*. He was killed by a drunk driver on his 75th birthday in 1992. He is buried near Sinatra in the Palm Springs Memorial Cemetery. The restaurant moved to 262 South Palm Canyon in 1974. It's now Wang's of the Desert.

From the 1972 Palm Springs Phone Directory.

Entryway to Sunmor Estates at the corner of
East Livmor Avenue and North Farrell Drive.

Central Palm Springs
Sunmor

East of Sunrise Way, you'll find a large section of moderate and upper middle class homes perfect for the folks who have attained a certain social status. These are the homes, built primarily in the 1950's and 60's by builders and designers with recognizable names like Alexander, Williams, Cody, Wexler and Frey and purchased by a hard working slice of society who have arrived to enjoy a very splendid bright spot in the desert. Even a particular man who was Mayor of Palm Springs more times than any other individual recognized the value in owning a home here.

You may very well be tempted to snap photos of really great mid-century modern homes that are part of Palm Springs Galaxy of Stars in their own right. But do you know what's weird? When I was a boy, these were simply the homes that everybody lived in. They weren't the desirable edifices of a modern age. They were just average and above average homes. It's nice to see the old stomping grounds become popular.

Sunmor is primarily a four or five block neighborhood tucked neatly behind City Hall. But, for our purposes, we'll let it encase parts of the Baristo neighborhood as well. So its borders shall be Sunrise Way on the west, the Palm Springs Airport on the east, Alejo Road on the north and we'll just cross over Ramon Road to the south.

At this point, though we've seen a lot, we're still not quite half way through Palm Springs pantheon of personalities.

Central Palm Springs: Sunmor

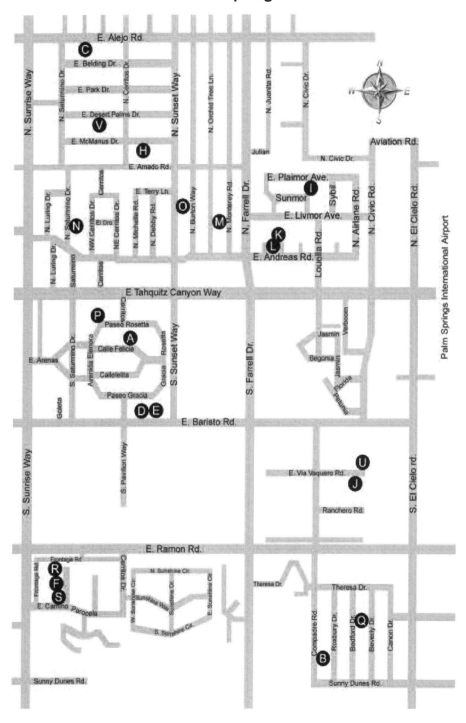

228

Ⓐ 2100 Calle Felicia

FRANK SCULLY

Variety columnist of "Scully's Scrapbook," who wrote an expose on a 1948 alien space crash in Arizona and Aztec, New Mexico bought this home in 1957. He died in this 1,288sf 3 bed 3 bath 1956 home in 1964. He was also a Papal Knight of the Order of Saint Gregory.

Ⓑ 660 South Compadre Road

A. ARNOLD GILLESPIE

Special effects pioneer, *North by Northwest, Forbidden Planet*, and more, specializing in miniatures who received 12 Oscar nominations lived here in 1964. The home was built in 1958 and has 3 bdrm 3 baths comprised of 1,682sf on a 10,454sf lot.

Ⓒ 1897 East Alejo Road

FERNANDO LAMAS

Argentinian heart throb, who was signed by MGM, this actor and his wife, Dahl, stayed in the 3 bed 2 bath home of local Realtor Ernest Dunlevie as a guest in 1956. The 1868sf home was built in 1956 and sits on a 10,019sf lot. Lamas was married four times, the last from 1969 till his death in 1982, was to actress Esther Williams.

Ⓓ 2122 East Baristo Road

THOMAS ARDIES

Newspaperman turned author who wrote a mystery thriller titled Palm Springs, lived here in 1978 and owned it till 1993. His widow owned it another 8 years till 2001. It's a 1,727sf home, built in 1960 with 3 beds 2 baths and sits on a 9,583sf lot.

Ⓔ 2300 East Baristo Road

CAMELOT THEATRE

Built in 1967 with a huge curvilinear screen 68 feet wide and thirty feet high was at the time billed "California's Most Modern Theatre." After closing in 1992 due to new theatre competition, it was reopened in 1999 as a showcase for independent films by Ric and Rosene Supple, the owners of KPSI, KDES and KNWZ under the name R & R Broadcasting.

Ⓕ 1740 East Camino Parocela

FRANK GORSHIN

Impressionist comedian and actor, most famous for his role as The Riddler in the 1960's *Batman* TV series, in 1996 lived in this 3 bed 3 bath 1,690sf 1973 condo. This address may be that of his publicist..

PAT MCCORMICK

The actor famous for his role as Big Enos Burdette in *Smokey and the Bandit I & II* lived in this condo in 1996 too.

⊞ 2155 East McManus Drive
TED GROUYA

Hollywood composer: Flamingo, In My Arms, and more, lived here in 1957. Home was built in 1955 and has 3 bedrooms 3 baths with 1,440sf on a 12,190sf lot. His son Ted Grouya, Jr. wrote, directed and produced Jerks.

① 2787 East Plaimor Avenue
FRANK BOGERT

Palm Springs Mayor, Thunderbird Country Club & El Mirador Hotel manager, horse wrangler, publisher and author of the book: Palm Springs First One Hundred Years, lived in the desert from 1927-2009. He died in the city he loved at the age of 99. The home was built in 1955. It has 4 bedrooms 3 baths with 2,383sf on a 13,068sf lot. It's now owned by his wife Negie.

Ⓙ 2949 East Via Vaquero Road
Harry Guardino

Stage and film actor lived here from 1998-2001. His ballerina widow Elyssa still owns this 1950 3 bed 2 bath 3,124sf home on a 17,424sf lot.

Ⓚ 231 Lyn Circle
George Alexander

Custom built in 1958 by Palm Springs mid-century modern builder etraordinairre George Alexander. It has 4 bedrooms and 4 baths with 2,550sf on a 9,583sf lot. The U-shaped home surrounds a pool and jacuzzi in the back yard.

Liberace

Famed pianist's second Palm Springs home. This was Liberace's guest house. His full name is Wladziu Valentino "Lee" Liberace.

L **212 North Jill Circle**

ROBERT LIPPERT, JR.

Second generation film producer of B movies, including *Sins of Jezebel* starring Paulette Goddard and *The Great Jesse James Raid* starring Barbara Payton and co-starring Tom Neal (both made in 1953), lived here in 1960. 3 bed 2 bath home was built in 1958, has 1,278sf on a 10,454sf lot.

M **247 North Monterey Road**

HUELL HOWSER

Host of PBS's travel show *California Gold*, who doggedly pursues the unique and obscure tourist destinations of California, bought this 1958 2 bed 2 bath 1,278sf home with a pool in 2000 and he still lives here.

Ⓝ 246 North Saturmino Drive

ANDREW MORGAN MAREE III

Tax accountant and financial advisor to many of the stars lived here in this 3 bedrooms 3 bathrooms 3,076sf 1957 home on a 15,246sf lot from 1992-2006.

◉ 266 North Sunset Way

HARPER GOFF

Harper began his Hollywood career with Warner Brothers as a set designer: *Charge of the Light Brigade*(1936) and more. But after running into Walt Disney in a London model shop where they both wanted to buy the same train, he became the Art Director for such films as *20,000 Leagues Under the Sea*(1954). Goff lived here in 1963. It's a modest 3 bed 2 bath home with 1728sf on a 10,890sf lot. He died in PS in 1993.

Ⓟ 2002 Paseo Roseta
SHEPPARD SANDERS

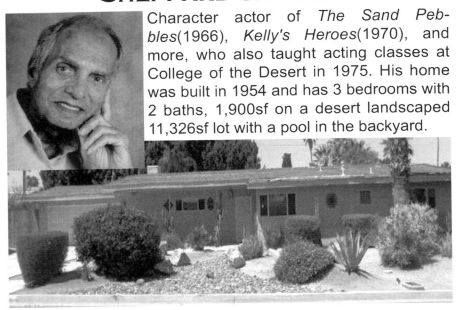

Character actor of *The Sand Peb-bles*(1966), *Kelly's Heroes*(1970), and more, who also taught acting classes at College of the Desert in 1975. His home was built in 1954 and has 3 bedrooms with 2 baths, 1,900sf on a desert landscaped 11,326sf lot with a pool in the backyard.

Ⓠ 613 South Beverly Drive
HARRIET PARSONS

Feminist producer of 47 titles including: *Screen Snapshots*(1930's), *Meet the Stars* (1940's), *Susan Slept Here*(1954), and more, bought this 3 bed 2 bath 1,858sf home new in 1958. It sits on a 10,454sf lot with a pool.

Ⓡ 1716 East Camino Parocela

FRED SCOTT

Singing cowboy actors' second residence in Palm Springs (1974-2001) where he lived with his wife Mary. It's a 2 bed 2 bath 1,119sf condo built in 1973. He lived here till his death in 1991. The condo remained in his family till 2001.

Ⓢ 1742 East Camino Parocela

DON DURANT

Tall, dark & handsome, western actor who played *Johnny Ringo, The Fastest Gun in the West,* on the CBS series by the same name, lived in this 3 bed 3 bath 1,690sf condo prior to 1994. It was built in 1973.

Ⓤ 2970 East Vaquero Road
BOB & DOLORES HOPE

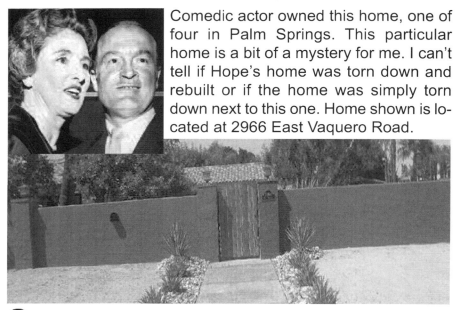

Comedic actor owned this home, one of four in Palm Springs. This particular home is a bit of a mystery for me. I can't tell if Hope's home was torn down and rebuilt or if the home was simply torn down next to this one. Home shown is located at 2966 East Vaquero Road.

Ⓥ 1961 East Desert Palms Drive
CONRAD HILTON

Hotel magnate owned this home till his death in 1979. It boasts 5 bedrooms 5 baths and has 4,286sf on a 20,038sf double lot and has two tennis courts.

From the 1963 Palm Springs Phone Directory.

Paul Pospesil Colllection

Lucille Ball and former PS Mayor Frank Bogert at the
Grand Opening of the Desi Arnaz Western Resort Hotel
and Golf Club in Indian Wells in 1957

Demuth Park

A collection of homes near Palm Springs largest public park. These properties were originally constructed, starting in the 1940's and 50's, at a time when the El Mirador Hotel was serving as a convalescent home for returning GI's after World War II and the builders of the day aptly named the development The Veterans Tract to attract buyers.

It's made up mostly of smaller ranch style homes. But due to an assortment of different builders and designers you'll find every style of home conceivable from modernistic to southwest to eastern seaboard. Mostly, this is where the working families of Palm Springs lived: tradesmen, shop owners, barbers and teachers. But it also attracted a few of the celebrities, including a particular big band singer, who wanted affordable housing Realtors shingle.

The park is a busy gathering place for the children of Palm Springs. It's the llargest collection of soccer and baseball fields in the city and many months of the year you'll find the streets clogged with passenger vehicles and SUV's on the weekends.

On the northern edge of the neighborhood, near Ramon Road and Gene Autry Trail there's a business district teeming with light industry: a mortuary, the Animal Shelter, an exotic car dealer, the Desert Water Agency and Knott's Soak City water park.

This is a section of the city though where good deals can still be found, where high value meets low price and like the citizens and celebrities of the past, the working class can invest in a spot where they can feel like retiring war hero's living in the midst of a land dotted with stars.

Demuth Park

Ⓐ 717 Mountain View Drive

ROBERT DIX

Actor who was most successful in cheap horror films by Al Adamson. This 1,565sf home was built in 1957. It has 4 bed 3 baths and sits on a 8,712sf lot. Dix was in 46 titles from 1954-73, including: *Forbidden Planet*(1956), *Young Jesse James*(1960), and *Live and Let Die*(1973).

Ⓑ 760 South Calle Santa Cruz

EADIE ADAMS

Big band singer lived here. The home was built in 1958 and has 3 bed 2 bath with 1,317sf and a 7,405sf lot. In 1962 Before she founded Eadie Admas Realty, Adams acted in 7 films between 1935-37 and sang I'd Be Lost Without You for the movie *Sinner Takes All*(1936).

© 975 South Paseo Dorotea
PAUL SAWTELL

Composer lived here for two years. It's a 3 bed 2 bath 1949 home with 1,614sf of space on a 12,197sf lot across the street from Demuth Park. Sawtell composed a massive 443 titles, including: *Comanche Station*('60), *Maverick*('59-61) and *Voyage to the Bottom of the Sea*('64-68)

Chi Chi

NIGHT CLUB & RESTAURANT

★ STARLIGHT ROOM ★
STAR ENTERTAINMENT
DINING & DANCING
BANQUETS FOR CONVENTIONS & SERVICE CLUBS

★ CHI CHI LOUNGE ★   ★ CRYSTAL ROOM ★
ENTERTAINMENT   EXCELLENT GOURMET
DANCING   CONTINENTAL CUISINE
COCKTAILS 11 A.M. 'til 2 A.M.   SPECIAL LUNCHEON & DINNERS
                                 11 A.M. 'til 12 MIDNIGHT

"DAILY DOW JONES NEWS SERVICE"
—— RESERVATIONS ——
325-1545

217 N. PALM CANYON DR.   PALM SPRINGS

From the 1966 Palm Springs Phone Directory.

Eric G. Meeks Colllection

Bob Hope, Frank Sinatra and Dean Martin
waiting for a tee time on June 10th, 1982

DEEP WELL HOTEL

24 ACRES OF DESERT WONDERLAND

*Deluxe Accommodations—
Rooms, Suites, Cottages*

**PEGGY WORKMAN'S
CONDITIONING
SALON FOR WOMEN**

**BATHS AND MASSAGE
SALON FOR MEN**

- **HEATED POOL** · **TENNIS COURTS**
- **BADMINTON** · **HORSE SHOES**
- **SHUFFLE BOARD** · **PING PONG**
  SWIMMING LESSONS

Coffee Shop
Ethyl's Hideaway
1020 E. Palm Canyon Drive
(HIGHWAY 111 TO INDIO)
PHONE 32 4-1371

From the 1963 Palm Springs Phone Directory.

Deep Well

In the 1920's a well was dug on this farm land to a depth of 630 feet, during a time of serious drought, and thereby feeding the existing orchards with much needed water; thus giving this section of Palm Springs its name. In 1928, the land was purchased by Charlie Doyle, who built a western style Dude Ranch with accommodations for 22 guests.

The ranch was bought and sold again and in the 1930's the owners expanded the enterprise to include construction of a few houses on steets named after horses: Palomino and Pinto.

But it wasn't until the 1940's when a designer named Paul Troesdale, from the Beverly Hills section of Los Angeles, coupled together with Bill Grant, who'd built the Thunderbird Country Club out of the Thuinderbird Dude Ranch in Rancho Mirage, looked for a new location to repeat his past successes. Deep Well Ranch became that place.

The emerging economy of the 1950's and the spotlight of celebrities brought new focus to Palm Springs. The droughts of the 1920's and the subsequent Depression Era was quickly passing by and Deep Well (sometimes spelled Deepwell) was in an opportune position to capitalize on a burgeoning market of second generation Hollywood stars and leaders of buiness who all wanted to partake of the world renown pleasantries known to exist in the formerly small desert town.

Palm Springs was growing up and the newest residents wanted large homes and large lots, close to the downtown corridor. Deep Well provided these urban pleasures with a uniquely Southwestern flair.

Deep Well

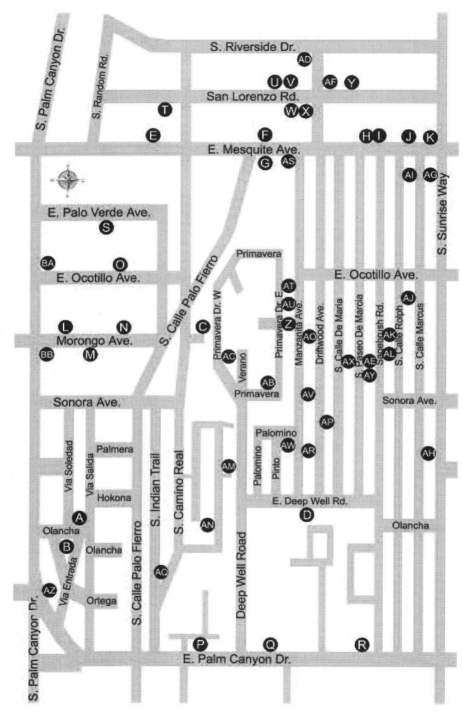

248

Ⓐ 360 Avenida Olancha
DON TOSTI

Bandleader, composer lived in this 2,787sf 3 bed 3 bath 1948 house from 1973 till his death in 2004. It sits on a 10,454sf lot. Tosti's career spanned several decades. He was best known for his "Pachuco" style of music. His song Pachuco Boogie was the first Latin single to sell a million records.

Ⓑ 238 Avenida Ortega/297 Avenida Olancha
MAX FACTOR, JR.

The son of the famous cosmetics company founder, Jr., was actually born with the name Frank Factor but family urged him to change it to Max Jr. He died in 1996. Home is now owned by Max's son Andrew Factor. Address was changed from 297 Avenida Olancha in 1974 when the home became apartments.

C 852 East Biltmore Place

MURRAY KORDA

Violinist lived here for 20 years although determining the exact years were inconclusive. There is a gap though in title records from when the 3 bedroom 3 bath 2,010sf home was built in 1957 to 1992. It sits on a 18,295sf lot with a pool.

D 1115 East Deepwell Road

HARRIET PARSONS

Feminist producer bought this 2 bed 2 bath home in 1955. It has 1,420sf of space on a 10,890sf lot. Parsons produced the *Screen Snapshot Series*(1935-40), *Meet the Stars series*(1940-41) and several movies including: *Joan of Ozark*(1942), *I Remember Mama*(1948) & *Susan Slept Here*(1955).

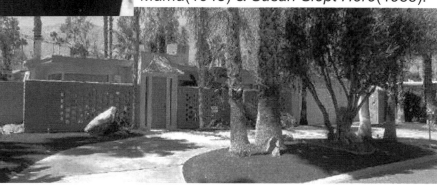

🄴 748 East Mesquite Avenue
PATRICK MACNEE

British "*Avenger*" actor purchased this home in 1973 and owned it till 1991. The 1,611sf home was built in 1952. It has 4 bedrooms and 2 baths with a 10,019sf lot and a pool and jacuzzi. MacNee played in 162 titles from 1938-2003 including: *The Howling*(1981) and *A View To a Kill*(1983).

🄵 1022 East Mesquite Avenue
RICHARD LANE

The voice of the LA roller derby team "Thunderbirds" and midget car racing, retired here in 1974. As a wrestling announcer in the 1950's & 60's he made up names, still in use today, for moves on the spur of the moment. This 2,081sf 1951 home has 3 bedrooms 3 bathrooms & a pool sunk into a 10,890sf lot.

Ⓖ 1139 East Mesquite Avenue

GINNY SIMMS

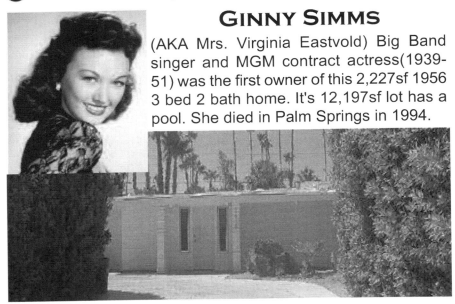

(AKA Mrs. Virginia Eastvold) Big Band singer and MGM contract actress(1939-51) was the first owner of this 2,227sf 1956 3 bed 2 bath home. It's 12,197sf lot has a pool. She died in Palm Springs in 1994.

Ⓗ 1422 East Mesquite Avenue

RUSSELL WADE

This is the second Palm Springs home of the RKO actor and real estate developer. He lived in this 3 bed 2 bath home in 1957. It was built in 1948 with 1,752sf on a 10,454sf lot. Wade acted in 79 titles from 1933-48) including: *Pirates of the Prairie*(1942) and *Beyond Glory*(1948)

❶ 1450 East Mesquite Avenue
ERIC G. MEEKS

Author, Palm Springs historian and former owner of Celebrity Bookstore bought this 3 bed 2 bath 1948 Troesdale home in 1999 and restored it to its original Vintage flair with internet earnings & his wife's guidance. The 2,400sf home sits on a 10,454sf lot. Please don't disturb the tenants.

❶ 1580 East Mesquite Avenue
CHARLES WINNINGER

Actor of 77 roles from 1915-60 including: *State Fair*(1945), *Science Fiction Theatre*(1955), more, retired here prior to his death in PS in 1969. His widow Gertrude Walker lived here writing mystery novels till her death in 1995. The 4 bed 3 bath 2,569sf 1948 home sits on a 10,454sf lot with a pool.

Ⓚ 1680 East Mesquite Avenue

RICHARD WHORF

Actor, who did 10 movie roles (1942-51) before switching to TV: *Perry Mason, The Untouchables, Gunsmoke, Wild Wild West,* and more, lived here till he died of a heart attack in 1966. The home was built in 1948. It has 4 bedrooms and 2 bathrooms, 2,107sf & a 10,454sf lot with a pool.

Ⓛ 156 East Morongo Road

SHARON TATE

Young actress lived here in 1961, the home of Roma Marvin, owner of La Roma Original Ladies Wear. Tate acted in 12 roles from 1961-67 including *The Beverly Hillbillies* and *Valley of the Dolls* before being murdered by the Manson Gang in 1969. The 1,821sf home was built in 1936, has 2 bdrm and 3 bath, and sits on a 10,890sf lot.

M 211 East Morongo Road
DR. WILLIAM SCHOLL

The original foot doctor (b.1882) built this 2,556sf Spanish-style 4 bedroom 4 bath home in 1941 and lived here till he died in 1968. Scholl began his career as a young shoe salesman in 1901, who cared so much for people's comfort he enrolled in medical school to better understand feet..

ROBERT H. COHN

Founder and Chairman of CFS Continental, a Chicago based food distribution company, bought this 4 bed 4 bath 2,556sf home in 1969. It was built in 1941 and sits on a 20,038sf lot.

N 646 East Morongo Road
ARTHUR LYONS

Mystery writer who co-wrote LA Coroner Thomas Noguchi's bestsellers: Unnatural Causes and Physical Evidence, depicting the autopsies of many celebrities lived in this 2,743sf 3 bedroom 3 bath 1950 home with his wife Barbara. Arthur died in 2008.

◎ 252 East Ocotillo Avenue

WILLIAM GRAY PURCELL

Mid-west architect who moved to the desert for therapeutic recuperation from tuberculosis built this 2 bedroom 3 bath home in 1935. It has 1,792sf of space and a lot of 10,019sf with a pool.

℗ 1000 East Palm Canyon Drive

BILTMORE HOTEL

Built in 1948. Designed by LA architect Frederick Monhoff. (Now Biltmore condominiums, shown here) This celebrity historied hotel operated for forty years until it closed down in 1988. The hotel was infamously known for foibles and troubles including: fire, food poisoning, kidnapping and a hoax terrorist bombing. I remember when I first moved here in 1976, the hotel had a small par 3 golf course along Hwy 111 and a huge bicycle rental company operated on the corner of Indian Avenue and Hwy 111.

From the 1963 Palm Springs Phone Directory.

Q 1050 East Palm Canyon Drive

BONITA GRANVILLE

Nancy Drew actress and her oilman husband Jack Wrather owned L'Horizon and lived onsite in 1954. She owned it till 1990. The hotel was designed by William F. Cody. Wrather also owned The Queen Mary and The Disneyland Hotel. Bonita and Jack co-produced Lassie on TV.

R 1400 East Palm Canyon Drive

LEO DUROCHER

(Joshua Tree Apartments, now Tennis Court Apartments) Baseball legend and manager of the New York Giants during their 1954 World Series Champion season, lived here in his retirement in 1976. During his career, he also coached the Dodgers, Cubs and Astros.

Ⓢ 245 East Palo Verde Avenue
SAM ZIMBALIST

Editor of 16 films: *Wizard of Oz*(1925), more. Producer of 25, *King Solomon's Mines*(1950) and *Mogambo*(1953), who died half-way through production of *Ben-Hur* in 1958. The 1,452sf home was built in 1940. It has 3 bedrooms and 2 baths and sits on a 10,019sf lot.

Ⓣ 777 East San Lorenzo Road
WERNER GROEBLI

(San Lorenzo Apartments) Frick of the 1940's and 50's Ice Capades comedy skating team Frick & Frack, with Hans-Rudi "Frack" Mauch. Life magazine called them "The Clown Kings of Ice." Groebli kept performing as a single into the 1970's.

Ⓤ 976 East San Lorenzo Road

WILLIAM WYLER

Producer of 71 films, Director of 15, who amassed forty Academy Awards with 128 nominations owned this home from 1951-1967. It was built in 1951, has 4 bedrooms and 3 baths in 1,539sf and a lot of 10,890sf. His works include: *Wuthering Heights*(1939), *Ben Hur*(1959) & *Funny Girl*(1968).

Ⓥ 1128 East San Lorenzo Road

WILLIAM A. SEITER

Director of 148 titles (1915-60) for film & TV including: *Laurel and Hardy: Sons of the Desert*(1933), Astaire and Rogers, the Marx Brothers, and many more. Seiter owned this 3 bedroom 3 bath 1949 home in 1951. It has 2,119sf of living space atop a 10,890sf lot.

W 1151 East San Lorenzo Road
DON HARTMAN

Writer, director, producer, Hartman owned this 3 bed 2 bath home which he called "Casa Sonrisa" in 1955. It was built in 1948 with 1,673sf of space and a 10,890sf lot. His works include: *The Road to Zanzibar*(1941), *It Had to Be You*(1947) with Ginger Rogers, & more.

X 1179 East San Lorenzo Road
PAUL TROESDALE

This is the same home as the one pictured above with Don Hartman.The two lots have been combined into one property. Troesdale is the Beverly Hills developer who, in partnership with PS pioneer Pearl McManus, built the Tahquitz River Estates homes. He lived here in 1956. The 3 bed 2 bath 1,947sf home was built in 1948 on a 10,890sf lot. These days, it has a pool.

1328 East San Lorenzo Road

BILLIE DOVE

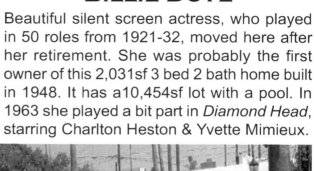

Beautiful silent screen actress, who played in 50 roles from 1921-32, moved here after her retirement. She was probably the first owner of this 2,031sf 3 bed 2 bath home built in 1948. It has a10,454sf lot with a pool. In 1963 she played a bit part in *Diamond Head*, starring Charlton Heston & Yvette Mimieux.

1302 Primavera Drive East

JOANNA MOORE

(Deepwell Ranch condominiums) Actress and mother of Tatum O'Neal lived here in 1980. It's a large 2 bedroom condo with 2,182sf of space on a 7,405sf lot. She played 91 roles from 1956-86. But is probably best known as Mayberry's Andy Taylor's girlfriend in 1960's season 3 of *The Andy Griffith Show*.

AB ## 1339 Primavera Drive East

RICHARD HORNER & LYNNE STUART

New York Theatre producer lived here with his wife, actress Lynne Stuart, from 1994 to 2002. Stuart's estate owned the 2 bed 2 bath 2,044sf condo till 2008. It was built in 1972 on a 7,405sf lot. Horner produced 70 plays on & off Broadway in nearly 40 years.

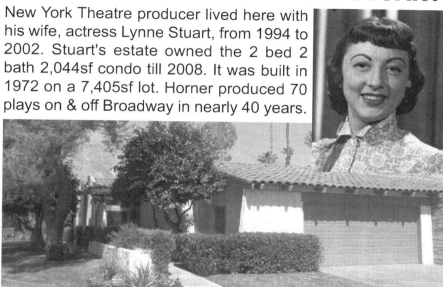

AC ## 1356 Primavera Drive North

VICTOR ORSATTI & MARIE MCDONALD

Talent agent and his showgirl wife Marie "The Body" McDonald lived here in 1975. The 2,044sf 2 bed 2 bath condo was built in 1970.

(AD) 1177 Riverside Drive North

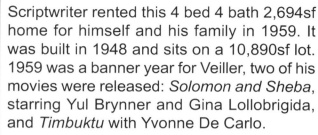

ANOTHONY VEILLER

Scriptwriter rented this 4 bed 4 bath 2,694sf home for himself and his family in 1959. It was built in 1948 and sits on a 10,890sf lot. 1959 was a banner year for Veiller, two of his movies were released: *Solomon and Sheba*, starring Yul Brynner and Gina Lollobrigida, and *Timbuktu* with Yvonne De Carlo.

(AE) 1349 Sagebrush Road

JERRY LEWIS

Comedic actor lived here from 1963 to 1975. The home was built in 1957 with 3 bdrms and 3 baths, 1,808sf of living space on a 10,890sf lot. These were prime years for Lewis. He made 20 films, beginning with *The Nutty Professor*, at this time, before taking an 8 year hiatus from Hollywood from 1972-1980.

AF ## 1228 East San Lorenzo Road

ANTHONY VEILLER

Scriptwriter who wrote *The List of Adrian Messenger*(1963) for Sinatra, Kirk Douglas and Tony Curtis while residing here in this 1948 home. It has 4 bedrooms and 3 baths with 2,876sf of space atop a 10,890sf lot. Veiller wrote 44 screenplays in his career.

AG ## 1070 South Calle Marcus

KENNETH TOBEY

In 1951, the actor of B Science Fiction and Horror films, who also portrayed Admiral Halsey in *MacArthur* lived in this 3 bed 3 bath 2,200sf home when it was new. Tobey played in 210 titles between 1945 and his death, in Rancho Mirage, in 2002.

1470 South Calle Marcus

WILLIAM H. PINE

Paramount producer lived here from 1952 till his death in 1955. It's a 1,710sf 3 bed 3 bath 1952 home on a 10,454sf lot with a pool. Pine made 80 movies over his 21 years, (1935-56), many of which are now considered classics, including *The Plainsman*(1936) & *Reap the Wild Wind*(1942).

 1044 South Calle Rolph

CARMEN MIRANDA

Miranda's second and last home in the desert. The home was built in 1951. It has 2 bedrooms and 2 bathrooms and a pool atop a 10,890sf lot. Miranda was in only18 roles from 1935-53 and yet made 35 soundtracks, some of which were made posthumously up until 2009. She died in 1955.

AJ 1280 South Calle Rolph
MARJORIE MAIN

Vaudeville, Broadway and film actress, who played in 89 titles from 1929-1964, yet was best known as Ma Kettle in the *Ma and Pa Kettle* movies. The 1948 home has 3 bedrooms and 3 baths in 1,869sf of living space atop a 10,454sf lot.

AK 1321 South Calle Rolph
ROBERT LIVINGSTON

Sci-fi & cowboy actor, who was in 137 roles from 1921-75, including: *The Three Mesquiteers*(1936), *Valley of the Zombies*(1946), more, retired to this home two years after it was built in 1950. The 1,459sf home has 2 bed 2 bath on a 11,326sf lot with a pool. His final three: *Girls For Rent*, & 2 *Stewardesses* films were horror-porno.

AL **1353 South Calle Rolph**

OSCAR G. MAYER

Yes, the hot dog king owned this 1,730sf 3 bed 3 bath house in 1955. It was built in 1950 atop a 11,326sf lot with a pool. Mayer took his grandfathers Chicago based meat processing company to be the nationally recognized leader in hotdogs and sandwich meats. He also invented the Weinermobile.

AM **1370 South Camino Real**

NINA WAYNE

Actress who played in seven roles from 1965-1973 including: *Bewitched*(1966(, *The Comic*(1969) starring Dick Van Dyke and *Love American Style*(1971) currently lives in this 2 bed 2 bath 1,163sf condo, built in 1973.

AN 1550 South Camino Real #222
RICHARD THORPE

MGM director retired to this 2 bed 2 bath 889sf condo sometime after it was built in 1974. Thorpe directed 185 titles from 1923-65 including: *The Great Caruso*(1951) with Mario Lanza, *Ivanhoe*(1952), and *Jailhouse Rock*(1957) starring Elvis Presley.

AO 1323 South Driftwood Drive
WILLIAM HOLDEN

Actor lived here from 1967-1977. The home is large by Palm Springs standards with 4,409sf, and 3 bdrms 4 baths. It has 4 lots combined into one gigantic property for a total of 42,253sf of land. Holden quickly became the leading man in his 74 roles (1938-81) including: *Sunset Blvd*(1950), *The Wild Bunch*(1969) and *Damien: Omen II*(1978).

1440 South Driftwood Drive

PHIL MOODY

Classical pianist has lived here since 1993. The home was built in 1955, has 5 bedrooms and 4 baths with 2,648sf of living space atop a 10,890sf lot and a pool. Besides his work at the keyboards for live performances, he also wrote three soundtracks for Hollywood. Moody died in PS in 2011.

 1620 South Indian Trail

VILLA ROYALE

Boutique hotel was at one time partially owned by actor Tony Shaloub (*Monk*) and his wife, actress Brook Adams. Villa Royale was also used once as a set for the TV series *MadMen* (season 2), when Don Draper took a hiatus with a 21 year old fling to find himself in SoCal and ended up in Palm Springs.

(AR) 1516 South Manzanita Avenue
WLADZIU LIBERACE

Famed pianist's first Palm Springs home, which he bought new in 1957. The 3 bed 4 bath 3,083sf home was built in1956 on a 10,890sf lot with a pool. Liberace owned four homes in Palm Springs. His mother owned another, as did his brother George.

(AS) 1075 South Manzanita Avenue
LORETTA YOUNG

Glamorous actress and her costume designer husband (Louis) bought his 3 bdrm 4 bath 1964 home in 1993. It has 3,510sf on a 12,197sf lot with a pool.Young began acting at age 4, in 1917, and performed her 107th role in 1994. She won an Oscar for *The Farmers Daughter*(1947) and an Emmy for *The Loretta Young Show*(1953).

Deep Well

 ## 1255 South Manzanita Avenue

JACK WEBB

The star of *Dragnet* lived in this 4 bed 4 bath 2,935sf home in 1965. The house was built in 1960 on a 10,890sf lot and has a pool. Webb didn't just act in his shows, he also wrote and Executive Produced them. Besides *Dragnet*, he also created, wrote or produced: *Emergency!, Adam-12*, and more.

1297 South Manzanita Avenue

JULIE LONDON

Singer of Cry Me a River and first wife of Jack Webb owned this 4 bedoom, 4 bath, 1954 home on a 10,890sf lot with a pool. In 1996, Julie and Jack's daughter Stacey was killed in a car wreck in Morongo Valley.

(AV) 1350 South Manzanita Avenue
THOMAS HULL

Las Vegas El Rancho hotel & casino owner and creator of The Vegas Strip lived in this 1959 home for the last four years of his life. He died in 1964. The home has 4 bdrms and 4 baths with 3,438sf of living space atop a 10,890sf lot with a pool and jacuzzi.

(AW) 1509 South Manzanita Avenue
EVA GABOR

Beautiful actress lived here in 1978. The home was built in 1958 with 2,734sf comprising 4 bedrooms and 4 baths. The lot is 10,890sf with a pool. At the time, Eva was married to her 5th hubbie, aerospace exec Frank Gard Jameson, Sr. and was doing TV series *Almost Heaven* and *Fantasy Island*.

1377 South Paseo De Marcia

BRIAN FOY

Oldest son of the *Seven lIttle Foys* and director of Ronald Reagan movies lived here in 1963. The 3 bed 3 bath 3,285sf 1962 home has a 11,326sf lot with a pool. As an adult, Foy produced 240 films, directed 57, wrote 10 and worked on 20. Best known: *House of Wax*(1953) with Vincent Price.

 1380 South Paseo De Marcia

FRANK SKINNER

Composer lived here in this 1,713sf 3 bed 2 bath home, built in 1954, with his lyricist wife, Grace Shannon, until his death in 1968. The home has a pool sunk into a 10,890sf lot. Skinner wrote music for 385 films during a 70 year career (1933-2009).

AZ ### 190 East Palm Canyon Drive

EVA GABOR DESIGN

Eva Gabor Design, an interior design studio. George Hamilton's younger brother **Bill Hamilton** greeted clients at the design studio. The location is now home to Joy Jacot Cabinets.

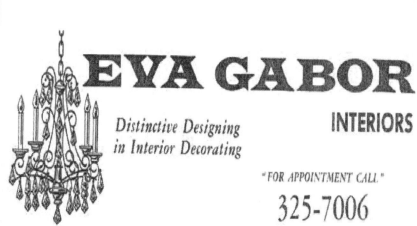

From the 1970 Palm Springs Phone Directory.

BA ## 1180 South Palm Canyon Drive

BOB LIPPERT'S STEAK HOUSE

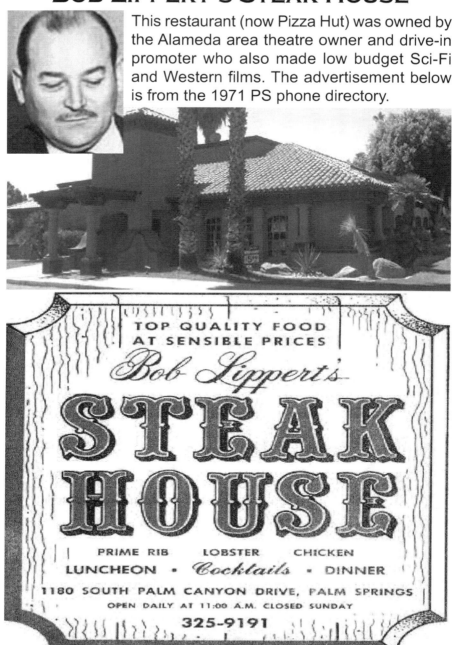

This restaurant (now Pizza Hut) was owned by the Alameda area theatre owner and drive-in promoter who also made low budget Sci-Fi and Western films. The advertisement below is from the 1971 PS phone directory.

TOP QUALITY FOOD
AT SENSIBLE PRICES

Bob Lippert's

STEAK HOUSE

PRIME RIB   LOBSTER   CHICKEN
LUNCHEON • *Cocktails* • DINNER
1180 SOUTH PALM CANYON DRIVE, PALM SPRINGS
OPEN DAILY AT 11:00 A.M. CLOSED SUNDAY
325-9191

BB 1342 East Palm Canyon Drive
CASA BLANCA MOTOR LODGE

Filmmaker, Al Adamson, and his busty actress wife, Regina Carrol, owned the Casa Blanca Motor Hotel (now the Musicland Hotel) where they housed over the hill actors and other assorted degenerates in the production of B grade horror sexploitation movies. Adamson, learned his filmmaking skills from his father, Victor, during the making of the film *Halfway to Hell*. He discovered Carrol and put her in the film *Psycho-a-Go-Go*(1965). One of Carrol's earliest films *The Female Bunch*(1969) was shot at the Spahn Ranch, where the Manson Family Gang was living and shortly after the filming concluded, Manson and his followers murdered Sharon Tate. In 1975, Adamson rented **899 North Avenida De Las Palmas,** in the Movie Colony neighborhood,

to make one of his same year films; most likely either *Naughty Stewardesses, Jessi's Girls,* or *Blazing Stewardesses*, with a slight possible chance it was *Black Heat*. Adamson went on to direct 30 films, 17 of them he produced himself. Carrol made 19. In 1995, Adamson's body was found murdered by his contractor live-in friend and buried under the jacuzzi of his Indio home. Carrol had died three years earlier, at only 49, of cancer.

Eric G. Meeks Colllection

Sonny Bono inspired a revival of Mesa area homes during his
life in Palm Springs. He was Mayor from 1988-92. This is a
publicity photo from Sonny's Congressional campaign in 1994.

Mesa

This cluster of homes, on it's winding streets and craggy precipices is magnificant blend of historic Palm Springs and its celebrity heritage.

Orignally subdivided by Los Angeles businessman Edmond Fulford, who also founded Palm Springs hardware enterprise Builders Supply on Sunny Dunes Road, many of this area's earliest homes were built in the 1930's and 40's. Some of them are even designated historical landmarks and others were entire compounds built by celebrities themselves as private retreats to house small herds of stars from the studio stables.

Fulford had a dream he never got to see come true. He envisioned a private gated neighborhood, where all residents entered via a single entrance. The only remnant of his vision is a single slump stone gate house which still stands on El Portal Drive between South Palm Canyon Drive and Mesa Drive. Still, I believe he would have been happy with the area's outcome. it's one of the most elite neighborhoods in town; benefiting from both the natural ambience of the least windy part of Palm Springs due to the rocky embrace of the steep face of Mount San Jacinto offering a seclusion from the desert elements.

The exclusivity provided by a unique geological location has been recognized for its natural beauty by moguls of film and pillars of the community alike, each have descended upon the rocky outcroppings to create their own level of nirvana in an otherwise desolate world, their own mesa upon which to perch their Adobe abode. The Mesa neighborhood allows the homeowners to be both close to town and close to nature.

Mesa

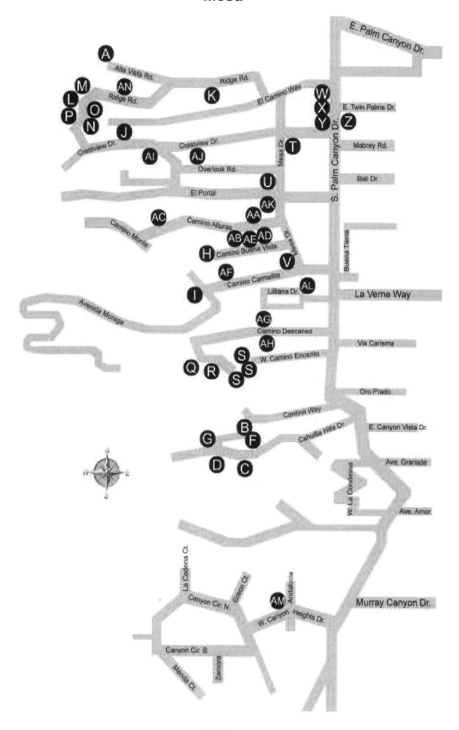

Ⓐ 385 Alta Vista Road
WRIGHT S. LUDINGTON

Heir apparent son of the owner of The Saturday Evening Post, Wright Saltus Ludington, built this home in 1938 and used it as a gay retreat in a time when reclusiveness was necessary for his lifestyle. The original building was a two-story European style villa with 5 bdrms and 4 bath with a large outdoor Greco-Roman bath.

LOUIS BENOIST

Best known as one of the 1960's owners of Almaden Wineries, Benoist bought this home in 1949. In 1950, he hired Albert Frey to build a guesthouse with a glass roof that had a canvas rolltop for shade and utilized natural hillside rock for the fireplace.

SUZANNE SOMERS & ALAN HAMEL

Actress, author, fitness guru and celebrity chef, with her husband Alan Hamel, bought the house in the late 1970's from the Benoist widow. These were the years of *Three's Company* and failed contract negotiations that ultimately ended with Somers departure from the show. So, to divert their attention, the couple enlarged the guesthouse with a bedroom suite, 2 offices and a guest wing to the main house. Somers went on to make a fortune with Gunthy-Renker(headquartered in Palm Desert) infomercials selling the Thighmaster device. In the 1990's, Somers and Hamel also applied for renovation permits to the upper land which accompanies the home, to be reconfigured as horse stables, but the City Council turned down the building application.

B 13 Cahuilla Hills Drive

LILY PONS & ANDRE KOSTELANETZ

International Opera star, Pons, owned this home with her husband/conductor, Kostelanetz, in 1956. It was built in 1955, has 4 bedrooms and 5 baths with 3,529sf on a 39,204sf lot. Pons made three movies for RKO studios from 1935-37, performed nearly 300 times for the NY Metropolitan Opera House and made dozens of records.

C 17 Cahuilla Hills Drive

JOLIE GABOR

Mother to Zsa Zsa, Eva & Magda Gabor. Jolie lived here for 40 years, while married to Count Odon "Edmund" De Szigethy, from when the home was new in 1958 till her death in 1997. After Odon's death in 1987, the three sisters bought the home. The 3 bd 3 bath home has 1,965sf on a 23,958sf lot.

D 19 Cahuilla Hills Drive
ZSA ZSA GABOR

Actress resided here in 1960 between marriages to actor/singer George Sanders(#3), and investor Herbert Hutner(#4). She was marrried a total of nine times. The home is a large 1 bed 2 bath dwelling, built in 1958 with 1,784sf on a 17,424sf lot with a small pool and a gazebo, a perfect spot to relax.

F 2401 Cahuilla Hills Drive
RIFAEL MARKOWITZ

Creater/Producer, Master of Ceremonies for, and owner of, The "Fabulous" Palm Springs Follies, lives in this 1,808sf 2 bed 2 bath hilltop 1999 home on a 55,321sf lot. Not sure if he bought it from, or it was built by, local developer and Palm Springs Fashion Plaza owner John Wessman.

Ⓖ 2429 Cahuilla Hills Drive

GEORGE MONTGOMERY

Cowboy actor built this modest 2 bed 2 bath 1,673sf home on a 19,602sf lot in 1966. Montgomery, the youngest of 15 siblings, played against Gene Autry in many early westerns. In 1958 he starred in his own TV series *Cimarron City*. Montgomery built 11 homes and there's a bronze statue of him near the Pickford Theatre in CC

Ⓗ 272 West Camino Buena Vista

JOEY ENGLISH

Radio talk show host, English, and her husband, Martin Botwinick, bought this expansive 8 bedroom 6 bath 3,215sf 1924 home on a 36,590sf lot in 1999. The home is PS Historic Site #48, as it magnificently represents the early rusticity of the city and was the home of PS City Councilman Earl Neel.

❶ 1995 Camino Monte

HOWARD DAVIDSON

The first owner of "Ship of the Desert," after it was built in 1937 by designers Adrian Wilson and Erle Webster for the Brigadier General (at the time Lieutenant Colonel), Davidson, who earned the Flying Cross for commanding the 10th Air Force in WWII in India. The home has 6 bedrooms and 5 baths with 2,636sf.

JACK L. WARNER

Owned by Warner in 1945 with his wife Anne Boyar. Youngest of the Warner Brothers.

❿ 301 El Camino Way/294 West Crestview Drive

SONNY & MARY BONO

Pop-icon, restaurateur, PS Film Festival founder, PS Mayor (1988-1992) and U.S. Representative for PS in 1994, till he died in a skiing accident. Sonny & Mary bought this estate in 1986. The 1940 home has 7 bdrm plus a 2 bdrm guesthouse, sits on a 1 & 1/2 acre lot with a pool. Mary sold it shortly after Sonny's death in 1998.

Ⓚ 275 Ridge Road

PAUL POSPESIL

Palm Springs celebrity photographer lived in this 3 bed 3 bath 2,529sf 1955 home till 1999. It has a secret bomb shelter basement built under it's 12,632sf lot. Paul worked in Palm Springs as a photographer for hire or a staff hotel photographer for over 50 years and can be found listed in the phone directory's of the 1950's. Several of my celebrity photographs were purchased from Paul. Born in 1917, he died in 2009 at 91 years old. His wife's name was Julie and his nickname was Popsicle.

Ⓛ 1716 Ridge Road

EDMUND GOULDING

One of four guest cottages built by Goulding and designed by actor/architect Tom Douglas in 1935, along with a little stone bridge across a terraced ravine to create the feel of a Cornish village. It's a 3 bed 2 bath with 1,178sf and, as with all of Gouldings homes, was sold to a studio boss. See page 303.

Ⓜ 1718 Ridge Road
EDMUND GOULDING

One of four guest cottages built by Goulding, designed by actor/architect Tom Douglas in 1935, along with a little stone bridge across a terraced ravine to create the feel of a Cornish village. This cottage sports a 3 car garage and was also sold to a studio boss.

Ⓝ 1752 Ridge Road
ANITA STEWART

Silent Screen Star built this 1937 home after retiring from acting in 1929. She acted in the first of her 99 roles in 1911 in *A Tale of Two Cities*. She produced 17 films during her career. The home is a 4 bed 4 bath 3,264sf dwelling on a 16.533sf lot with a pool.

1752 Ridge Road continues...

1752 Ridge Road continued...

EDMUND GOULDING

First of three Palm Springs homes bought by the Biritish director, writer, composer in 1938 and dubbed "The Little White House." Goulding wrote 66 films, directed 41. Best known for *Grand Hotel*('32) & *Nightmare Alley*('47), and he only became a director after writing the book Fury & MGM took a chance on him.

STUDIO BOSS

A studio boss bought all of Gouldings properties in one fell swoop, most likely to help Goulding switch from merely director to producer. The boss used them as an actor's retreat to reward the best members of his stable. See page 303 for more info.

CLARK GABLE

Gable stayed here during his rising star years and shortly after being the scoundrel Rhett Butler in *Gone With the Wind*. This was also the years that Gable was seeking a divorce from 2nd wife, Ria Langham, while dating Carole Lombard, who died in a plane crash('42).

B. DONALD BUD GRANT

President of CBS Entertainment(1980-87), with his wife Linda, bought this home in 1996 and owned it till 2004. Grant was a NBC daytime programmer who started his TV career in 1956, helped developed *Days of Our Lives*, and rose thru the ranks.

◎ 1755 Ridge Road

EDMUND GOULDING

One of four guest cottages built by Goulding and designed by actor/architect Tom Douglas in 1935, along with a little stone bridge across a terraced ravine to create the feel of a Cornish village. Eventually this was sold to a studio boss as an actors retreat. See page 303 for more information on these homes.

Ⓟ 1765 Ridge Road

EDMUND GOULDING

One of four guest cottages built by Goulding and designed by actor/architect Tom Douglas in 1935, along with a little stone bridge across a terraced ravine to create the feel of a Cornish village. This home, along with 1755, 1752, and 1716 Ridge Road are all on a Private Road. See page 303 for more.

Mesa

Ⓠ 2145 South Camino Barranca

JERRY WEINTRAUB

From 1975-1997, the concert promoter and movie producer lived here. The 2,564sf home was built in 1945. It has 5 bedrooms 5 baths and sits on a 28,750sf lot. Weintraub is best known for *Oh God!*(1977), *Diner*(1982) *Karate Kid I, II, & III*, and *Ocean's 11, 12, & 13*.

Ⓡ 2165 South Camino Barranca

FRANK LLOYD

Producer-director lived in this 1955 2 bed 3 bath home with a pool in 1975. It has 1,583sf on a 10,454sf lot. Lloyd directed 134 films from 1914-55, produced 29, wrote 42 & acted in 63. Best known for: *Mutiny on the Bounty*(1935) with Clark Gable & *Blood on the Sun*(1945) starring James Cagney.

Ⓢ 2196 South Camino Barranca
WALTER LANG

Hollywood director of musicals owned this hilltop home in 1961. It was built in 1935 and has 8 bedrooms 6 baths, 9,768sf and sits on a 148,540sf lot with a pool and a rock embedded scenic parapice to overlook South PS.

BARRY MANILOW

Singer/songwriter bought this home in 1995 and then purchased several other homes and relandscaped them to form a single large compound with several entrance and exit points simultaneously allowing friends and family a degree of privacy and creating back exits just in case the paparrazi should converge on him.

MANILOW: 2194 & ? South Camino Barranca

Two small homes most accessible from Camino Barranca. 2194 is the only one visible from the street and appears to be a 1 bed 3 bath home of 1,890sf. It was bought by Manilow's boyfriend Garry C. Kief in 1999. 2197 is probably a studio.

The Manilow Estate continues...

MANILOW: 2140 South Camino Barranca

A rear entrance to the Manilow Estate. The stucco pillared wall surrounds the entire property.

MANILOW: 197 West Camino Encanto

This is a 1945 4 bedroom 4 bath home with 2,503sf on a 21,780sf lot that Manilow added to his PS holdings in 2006 and deeded to the Barney Trust. As with all of the Manilow Estate buildings, it's a red tiled Spanish Colonial style home with a smooth white stucco exterior finish.

MANILOW: 200 West Camino Encanto

I could not find any data on this address. But it appears to be a two or three bedroom Spanish stuccoed, red-tiled roof home, perhaps from a garage conversion.

T ## 1810 South Mesa Drive

LOU COSTELLO

Comedic actor lived here in this 2 bed 2 bath 2,250sf home in 1948, the same year he & his partner Bud Abbott met Frankenstein on the big screen. Costello made 49 films and produced 6 from 1926 till he died in 1959. The 1926 home is on a 10,454sf lot.

U ## 1885 South Mesa Drive

IRWIN RUBENSTEIN

Owner of The Dunes - often referred to as Ruby's Dunes - and married to singer Connie Barlow. He was a good friend of Frank Sinatra. Nancy Sinatra referred to him as "Uncle Ruby." He called this 5 bed 4 bath 2,724sf home with a pool "Villa Nirvana West." It was built in 1952 on a 16,988sf lot.

1993 South Mesa Drive

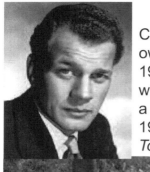

JOSEPH COTTEN

Cotten and his wife, actress Patricia Medina, owned this home, "White Gables," from 1985-1992. It was built in 1935, has 4,144sf with 3 bdrms 4 baths on a 28,314sf lot with a pool. Cotten acted in 132 shows between 1937-1981, including: *Citizen Kane*(1941), *Tora! Tora! Tora!*(1970), & more.

 ## 1701 South Palm Canyon Drive

MOORTEN BOTANICAL GARDEN

Stuntman Chester "Cactus Slim" Moorten and his wife, Patricia, opened this desert horticulturists dream garden in 1955. Their first nursery was at the corner of Indian Avenue and Tahquitz Canyon Way in 1938. Moorten worked, under the name Chester Morton, on the films *The Flaming Youth*(1927) with W.C. Fields and *The Sideshow*(1928) with Marie Prevost. When Chester and Patricia were married, James Edwards, of Edwards Theatres, was his best man.

⊗ 1735 South Palm Canyon Drive

STEPHEN H. WILLARD

"Touring Topics" Scenic photographer lived in this 2 bed 2 bath 2,096sf home, built in 1926 on a 19,166sf lot. Willard was born in 1894 and started taking pictures at 16. After WWI he moved to Palm Springs and opened his first studio where he would hand tint the enlarged spectacular photos. After his death in 1966, his collection was donated to the PS Desert Museum.

Ⓨ 1757 South Palm Canyon Drive

REGINALD OWEN

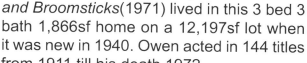

British character actor whose highlights include *Mary Poppins*(1964) and *Bedknobs and Broomsticks*(1971) lived in this 3 bed 3 bath 1,866sf home on a 12,197sf lot when it was new in 1940. Owen acted in 144 titles from 1911 till his death 1972.

1788 South Palm Canyon Drive

GEORGE JESSEL

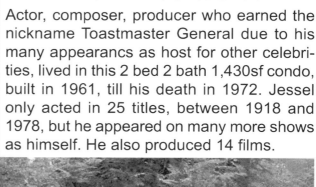

Actor, composer, producer who earned the nickname Toastmaster General due to his many appearancs as host for other celebrities, lived in this 2 bed 2 bath 1,430sf condo, built in 1961, till his death in 1972. Jessel only acted in 25 titles, between 1918 and 1978, but he appeared on many more shows as himself. He also produced 14 films.

 246 West Camino Alturas

LAWRENCE MARIO GIANNINI

Son of the founder of Bank of America, Lawrence (who went by Mario) built this 4 bedroom 3 bath 2,128sf home in 1946 as part of his retirement plan. He, unfortunately, died two years before his sixtieth birthday, before he could permanently occupy the home.

AB 259 West Camino Alturas

PANDRO S. "PAN" BERMAN

Producer of 115 films (1931-70) lived here in 1951. The home was built in 1945 with 5 bdrm 5 bath 2,576sf on a 13,504sf lot. Berman is best known for *National Velvet*('44), *Father of the Bride*('55), Elvis's *Jailhouse Rock*('57) and *A Patch of Blue*('65)

BILL GOODWIN

Actor bought this home in 1956. But on May 9th, 1958 he was found dead in his car late at night on South Palm Canyon Drive and his actress/wife Phillipa Hilber said he'd left a note saying he didn't feel well and had gone for a drive. Goodwin acted in 43 films from 1935-58, including: *Riding High*(1943), *Lucky Me*(1954) and *Bundle of Joy*(1956).

297

AC **366 West Camino Alturas**

JIM AND TAMMY FAYE BAKKER

Televangelists rented this 2,833sf 4 bedroom 4 bath 1958 home with a 25,700sf lot, called "Les Petit Oasis," in January 1988. It was from this home that the Bakkers tried to perpetrate a west coast religiously themed amusement/condominium and timeshare theme park similar to their fraudulently oversold Heritage Park idea which landed Jim in jail.

AD **244 West Camino Buena Vista**

ROBERT STACK

Stack's mother's home in 1955. It was built in 1945 with 3 bedrooms and 4 baths and a total of 2,574sf of space on a 10,890sf lot. Best known for playing Eliot Ness on TV's *The Untouchables*(1959-63), Stack acted in 95 titles from 1939-2003. Funniest role: *Airplane*('80).

AE 256 West Camino Buena Vista

SONNY BONO & CHER

Bought in the early 1970's while the musician & actor was still married to Cher. The 3 bed 3 bath home was originally built in 1945. It has 2,809sf with a 13,989sf lot. Sonny & Cher divorced in 1975; 1 daughter Chastity(Chaz). He sold it in Aug. of 1986.

AF 282 West Camino Carmelita

JOHNNY MERCER

Lyricist/composer lived in this 5 bedroom 3 bathroom home with his dancer wife, Ginger Meehan, and their kids. Mercer started writing songs for Hollywood in 1935 and wrote more than 1,500 before he died in 1976. Moon River, Jeepers Creepers, and more.

AG 242 West Camino Descanso

FAYE BAINTER

Best Supporting Actress for *Jezebel* lived here the year she won the Oscar in 1958. The home was built in 1940 with 3 bedrooms and 5 baths and 4,237sf of interior space on a 16,238sf lot with a pool and jacuzzi. Other works include: *Our Town*(1940) and *The Children's Hour*(1961).

AH 301 West Camino Descanso

RITA HAYWORTH

Silver screen actress lived here in the late 1970's and early 1980's. Records on this home were not easily available because in 2000 it burned to the ground in an electrical fire and had to be rebuilt. Hayworth acted in 65 films from 1934-72. She's best known for *Gilda*(1946), *The Lady From Shanghai*(1947) and *Pal Joey*(1957) with Sinatra.

AI 303 West Crestview Drive
ROBERT WAGNER

Actor purchased it in 1968 and then honeymooned here with Natalie Wood on their second attempt at marriage in 1972. The main house has 5 bedrooms and the second house, nearer the pool, has 3 bedrooms. They were first married in 1957.

HERMAN WOUK

Best-selling author of The Caine Mutiny('51), Marjorie Morningstar('55), The Way God Talks('10) & more, is the homes current owner.

AJ 277 West Crestview Dr./324 West Overlook Rd
KING CAMP GILLETTE

Also known as 324 West Overlook Road. The shaving razor magnate built this home in 1932. The estate is comprised of two homes: a 3 bedroom house with a 1,300sf reception room, a 3 car garage and stone fireplaces & a 1 bedroom guest house.

AK ## 235 West El Portal

LOUIS & JUNE HAYWARD

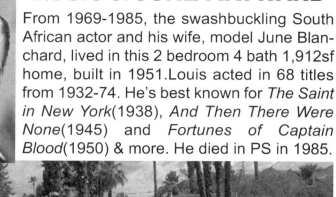

From 1969-1985, the swashbuckling South African actor and his wife, model June Blanchard, lived in this 2 bedroom 4 bath 1,912sf home, built in 1951.Louis acted in 68 titles from 1932-74. He's best known for *The Saint in New York*(1938), *And Then There Were None*(1945) and *Fortunes of Captain Blood*(1950) & more. He died in PS in 1985.

AL ## 230 West Lilliana Drive

RAYMOND CHANDLER

Mega-mystery author who penned the Palm Springs parody Poodle Springs while residing here. The home was built in 1955. It has 3 bedrooms 3 baths with 2,999sf and a 16,117sf lot with a pool. Other works include: Farewell, My Lovely, The Little Sister, more.

2851 West Andalucia Court

BETSY DUNCAN

Child actress who later married In-Sink-Erator Manufacturing company founder lives in this 4 bed 3 bath 2,896sf 1980 condo.

 356 Ridge Road

EDMUND GOULDING

The 1936 home is a 3 bed 2 bath with 1,002sf on a 15,682sf lot. The present owner of the home says it was formerly owned by a studio mogul who used it as an actors retreat and that it was a haven for Cary Grant. I feel it was originally built by Edmund Goulding as his main house while he built his Cornish village further back along Ridge Road and then the entire compund was sold to a studio boss. My research is incomplete on the properties of Edmund Goulding. I see work ahead for the 2nd edition of PS Celebrity Homes.

1955 Palm Springs Phone Directory Advertisment

South Palm Springs
Smoke Tree

Named for the home development on the south end of town, the stables, the home association and the shopping center give this section of Palm Springs its name.

Smoke Tree's 80 ranch-style homes was the impetus for it all. Originally built in 1936, it wasn't until the Markham family took over in 1945 that the association really took off with a western flair; dirt roads, barbed wire, wooden rail fences and horse back riding, were the norm and the donning of cowboy hats, Levi's and flannel shirts were often seen worn by the corporate elite and A-List stars around the rough hewn long wooden tables at chow time. It was a place where urban families could enjoy a throwback to simpler times.

This chapter of the book actually only includes a small survey of streets and celebrities. But the cadre of stars is strong and their influence was felt during the end of the Golden Era of Palm Springs and continued into the growing years of the 1960's, 70's and 80's. These days the streets are well trodden and the businesses established.

A few directors, a singer turned actor, and the suicidal daughter of one of Hollywood's greatest studio bosses will meet you here easily.

Truth be told, this is one chapter of the book I could use some assistance. I know more business leaders and stars who lived behind the gate of Smoke Tree deserve mention. But I've yet to truly crack this small but significant part of town. if you know of any information worthy of note, please contact me at meekseric@hotmail.com

South Palm Springs: SmokeTree

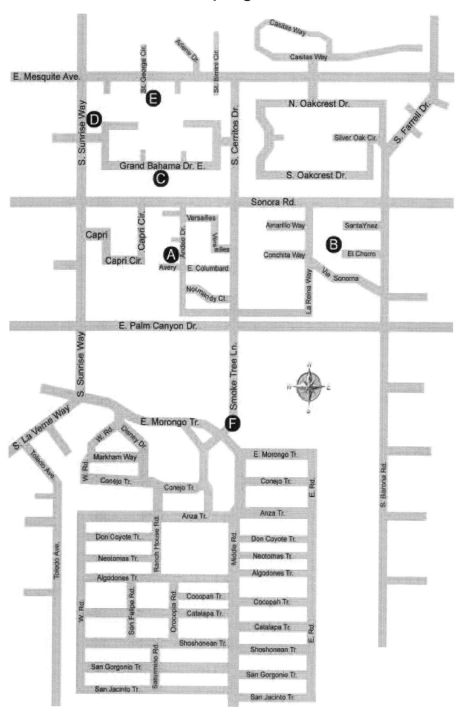

Ⓐ 1643 Andee Drive
A EDWARD SUTHERLAND

Paramount director, former Keystone Kop, and on-site owner of the Calypso Apartments, built in 1960. Sutherland,a lifelong friend of W.C. Fields, worked himself up from stage hand to actor,(44 films) director(58 films) & producer(7 films) who died in PS in 1973.

Ⓑ 2320 East El Chorro Way
SUSAN ZANUCK

The gay second daughter of Darryl F. Zanuck, who dated Rock Hudson, killed herself here on June 10, 1980 with an overdose of prolonged drinking and drug use. The 1,885 sf home was built in 1971. It has 3 bedrooms and 3 baths and sits on a 10,890sf triangular shaped lot with a pool in the backyard. Her father had died only 6 months earlier at Desert Hospital. Susan's daughter, Darrilyn, inherited the bulk of the family's fortune.

© 1971 Grand Bahama Drive East

FRANTISEK DANIEL

Writer(14 films), director(2 films), producer(1), lived in this 1,576sf 3 bedroom condo, built in 1972, from 1994 till his death in 1996. A Czech film maker, in America his greatest contribution was as a teacher of the dramatic arts, though his 1968 film *A Shop on Main Street* won an Oscar for Best Foreign Film. Daniel died in PS at the age of 69.

① 1700 Grand Bahama Drive West

OSCAR BRODNEY

Screenwriter lived here in 1975. Three bedroom, two bath 1,576sf condo was built in 1972. Brodney wrote 59 films and shows from 1942-1987, including: *Harvey*(1950) starring Jimmy Stewart, Two of the *Francis The Talking Mule* Movies starring Donald O'Connor, *The Glenn Miller Story*(1954), and TV series *Death Valley Days*(1960) and *It Takes a Thief*(1969-70).

Ⓔ 1012 St. George Circle

TENNESSEE ERNIE FORD

(Sunrise Villas Condominiums) Singer of "Sixteen Tons" lived here in retirement in 1980. Ford was a radio star, actor, singer and songwrter. He was nominated twice for Emmy Awards and has three stars on the Hollywood Walk of Fame.

Ⓕ 1850 Smoke Tree Lane

SMOKE TREE RANCH

These celebrity homeowners lived in Smoke Tree Ranch and I have yet to pinpoint the exact address and/or date:

I) **Dorothy Bekins**-Bekins Moving Company

II) **Walt Disney**-Smoke Tree has two Disney homes. One he built in 1948 and the other in 1957.

III) **Fred Gottschalk**-Owner of Gottschalk department stores

IV) **C.C. Knudsen**-Knudson Dairies

V) **George Murphy**-California Senator, actor, dancer, & former Vice-President of Desilu Studios.

VI) **Paul Troesdale**-Deep Well builder lived here in 1951.

The diagonal angling road which begins on the bottom left of this picture and proceeds upwards and to the right before becoming horizontal is LaVerne Way. It separates the Twin Palms neighborhood from the Canyon Country Club.

South Palm Springs
Canyon Cuntry Club & Twin Palms

For the purposes of this chapter, we're going to cover two established neighborhoods in one fell swoop.

At the entry to this part of town is Twin Palms. It's a development started by George and Robert Alexander with some 60 large and simple post and beam designed estates on large lots. They hired architects William Kriesel and Daniel Palmer for these significant structures and writers, actors and more snapped them up.

Then there's the Canyon Country Club; a huge development of Florida style homes and condos stretching from LaVerne Way to the Cahiulla reservation and is home to one of the most beautiful golf courses on the western end of the Coachella Valley. The Indians knew this to be pristine land and that's why there own best homes dot the edges of the valley here nestled nicely between the foothills of the Santa Rosa mountain range and the glorious heights of Mount San Jacinto.

This picturesque playground will engage you for hours. This is the best neighborhood for seeing quality A-List celebrities up close and personal. The homes are seldom behind ivy covered walls or prison like gates. You can see how they lived on a day to basis, witness their front yards, front doors ad drivewways. It'll be easy to imagine them waking up in the morning and stepping out front in nothing but a bathrobe, coffe in hand, grabbing the morning Desert Sun paper. And if you're extrmely lucky, you might just get to see an actual star themselves. Many of them still live in this pristine neighborhood of fine homes.

South Palm Springs: Canyon Country Club & Twin Palms

A 203 Aladdin Street

PETER M. THOMPSON

(Sahara Park Mobile Homes) Cowboy actor who worked on TV's *Santa Fe*(1951), *The Lone Ranger*(1955) and *Death Valley Days*(1956-57), lived here till death from a local traffic accident in 2001. Thompson acted in 40 titles from 1947 till his last film, *Monster-A-Go-Go* in 1965.

B 2370 Alhambra Drive

GENE BARRY

Actor of TV's *Bat Masterson* fame bought this 2 bed 3 bath home in 1975. It was built in 1968 with 2,765sf on a 12,635sf lot. Barry worked on 85 projects during his career, which began in 1950 with TV's *The Clock*. He also played in both *War of Worlds* films (1953 and 2005).

C **2410 Alhambra Drive**

TEDDY HART

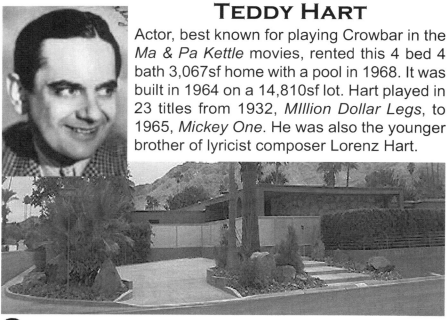

Actor, best known for playing Crowbar in the *Ma & Pa Kettle* movies, rented this 4 bed 4 bath 3,067sf home with a pool in 1968. It was built in 1964 on a 14,810sf lot. Hart played in 23 titles from 1932, *MIllion Dollar Legs*, to 1965, *Mickey One*. He was also the younger brother of lyricist composer Lorenz Hart.

D **1852 Apache Drive**

EDWARD DMYTRYK

Director who was a card carrying member of the Communist Party and one of the "Hollywood Ten," who was blacklisted during the McCarthy era hearings in 1951, bought this home brand new in 1957. It sits on a 12,362sf lot with 3 bedrooms and 2 baths enclosed in 1,600sf of living space.

E 1033 East Sierra Way

VAL & YOLANDE GUEST

Writer-director-producer known for 1950's science fiction films and the James Bond spoof *Casino Royale* with Peter Sellers. Guest lived in this 2 bdrm 3 bath 1969 home with actress-author wife, Yolande Donlan, till his death in 2006. Donlan still lives in the 2,772 sf home today.

F 1099 East Sierra Way

RALPH YOUNG

Singer and half of the duo Sandler and Young, lived here till his death in 2008. His widow still owns the 4 bed 4 bath 3,017sf home which was built in 1970 on a 13,504sf lot. Young is shown here on the left. He died in his Palm Springs home on August 22, 2008, at the age of 90.

Ⓖ 117 East Twin Palms Drive

MILTON KRASNER

Oscar winning cinematographer at one time owned this 2 bed 2 bath 1,289sf condo. Krasner started his film career in 1933 and worked on 160 projects, including being Director of Photography for *The Seven Year Itch* starring Marilyn Monroe(1955), and up until he retired after TV's *Columbo* in 1976.

Ⓗ 243 East Twin Palms Drive

MICHAEL "M.C." LEVEE

In 1961, this agent extraordinaire claimed to be President of The Royal Hawaiian Estates and sold two condominiums in an extravagant, nearly fraudulent, full-page newspaper campaign. Levee was one of the 36 founding members of the Academy of Motion Pictures Arts and Sciences and was the Acadmey's President from 1931-32. He began his career as a prop man for The Fox Film Corporation in 1917 and died in PS in 1972.

1549 East Twin Palms Drive
JOHN AYLESWORTH

in 1980, comedy writer Aylesworth owned this 2 bed 3 bath 2,690sf condo which was built in 1976. Aylesworth was a writer on 41 shows and films from 1962-92 and he produced 14 TV shows during that time, including *The Sonny and Cher Show*. Here he is shown with Lorne Greene of *Bonanza* fame.

1255 East Via Estrella
JEROME FACTOR

President of Max Factor Cosmetics, and cousin to Max, had this 3 bed 3 bath 5,471sf home built on a 24,394sf lot in 1969. Jerome's father John, known as Jake the Barber and half brother to the cosmetics company founder Max Factor Sr., was a Prohibition-era gangster and con man with the Chicago outfit.

Ⓚ 2627 Kings Road West
DOROTHY HART

Widow of Teddy Hart moved to this 2,899sf 3 bed 3 bath condo, built in 1968, after her husbands death in 1971. Teddy Hart was best known for playing the Indian Crowbar in the *Ma & Pa Kettle* movies and he was the brother of lyricist.composer Lorenz Hart.

Ⓛ 955 La Jolla Road
EDDIE FISHER & DEBBIE REYNOLDS

Actor, singer purchased this home when it was new in 1957 with his wife actress Debbie Reynolds after they married. It's a 3 bed 2 bath 1960sf home with a 12,197sf lot. The couple were married in 1955. But Fisher dumped Reynolds for Elizabeth Taylor and she and Reynolds had a feud that lasted past 2000.

Ⓜ 985 La Jolla Road
DONALD WOODS

Actor, not the B-picture movie producer, lived here in 1966. The 1957 home has 3 bedrooms and 2 baths with 1,600sf and a 10,890sf lot. Woods played in 137 roles from 1928-84, including: *The Return of Rin Tin Tin*(1947),TV series *Craig Kennedy, Criminologist*(1952) & *True Grit*(1969)

Ⓝ 1967 Ledo Circle
JAMES R. WEBB

Screenwriter lived here when he died in 1974. The home was built in 1970 with 3 bdrm 3 bath in 2,424sf of living space on a 10,454sf lot. Webb is best known for *The Big Country*(1958), *Cape Fear*(1962) and *How The West Was Won*(1962).

◎ 1380 Malaga Circle

HELEN ROSE

Costume Designer for 20th Century Fox & MGM, who designed Grace Kelly's wedding dress, lived here in 1978. It's a large 3 bed 3 bath 2,593sf condo, built in 1971, on a 3,920sf lot. She died in Palm Springs in 1986.

℗ 1570 Murray Canyon Drive

IRVING MILLS

Music publisher and composer lived in this 2 bed 5 bath home till he died in PS in 1985. The 4,052sf home was built in 1976. It sits on a 13,939sf lot. Mills Publishing Company either discovered or enhanced the careers of Hoagy Carmichael, Duke Ellington, Cab Calloway, Benny Goodman and many more.

ⓠ 1578 Murray Canyon Drive
GINNY SIMMS

Actress Simms (AKA Virginia Eastvold) died from a heart attack in this home on April 4, 1994. Her son producer/hotelier Conrad Von Dehn died here in 1995. Her husband, developer Donald Estvold died here a few years later. The home was sold in 2008.

ⓡ 1829 Navajo Circle
LEIF HENIE

Costume designing brother to 1928, 1932, & 1936 Olympic Figure Skating champion Sonja Henie. Leif and his second wife, Sally Weihle, bought this 2,200sf home new in 1957. It has 3 bdrms and 2 baths with a 10,890sf lot. Leif is shown here with Sonja.

Ⓢ 1841 Navajo Circle

ROBERT BUCKNER

Novelist, screenwriter and producer owned this 1957 4 bed 3 bath home with 1,600sf on a 10,454sf lot. Buckner wrote 40 films and TV shows including: *Knute Rockne*(1940), *Yankee Doodle Dandy*(1942), & *Bonanza*(1970).

Ⓣ 1877 Navajo Circle

DON FEDDERSON

Producer of *My Three Sons* and creator of *Family Affair* lived here with his second wife, actress Yvonne Lime. The 3 bed 4 bath 2,430sf home was built in 1957 on a 10,019sf lot with a pool. Fedderson also syndicated *The Lawrence Welk Show* till 1982, after ABC's cancelling of the series in 1971.

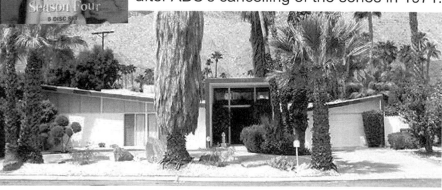

U 190 Sahara Street
JEAN CARSON

(Sahara Park Mobile Homes) Actress retired here until her death in 2005. Carson was in 61 titles from 1949-77, including: *I Married a Monster From Outer Space*(1958), *The Twilight Zone*(1960), *The Andy Griffith Show*(1962-65), and many more.

V 457 San Jose Road
MONTY HALL

Host of *Let's Make a Deal* at one time owned this 3 bed 2 bath 1,684sf Canyon View Estates condo. It was built in 1963 on a 3,049sf lot. Hall hosted and produced *Let's Make a Deal* from 1963-99. Early in his career he hosted other other games and was the commentator for the New York Rangers(59-60).

1837 South Caliente Road

RAY BRADBURY

Sci-Fi and weird tales author and his wife Marguerite, owned this 1,733sf 3 bed 2 bath desert home from 1981 till 2011. Bradbury began his writing career on a rented type-writer in the basement of UCLA's Powell Library. In all, he wrote 11 novels and over 400 novellettes and short stories.

As a young man, Bradbury was enthralled with magic and circuses. At one circus, he was invited on stage by a Mr. Electrico who, using his electrically lighted sword, knighted the young author to be with the words, "Live Forever." Bradbury was 92 when he died in 2012.

During his years in Palm Springs I was fortunate to meet Ray several times. He spoke at my PSHS graduation in 1983, reciting a story about a time-traveller who supposedly returned to his own time to tell the people about a beautiful future of clean living and spectacular edifices just 100 years away. The people built the future the traveller saw and when 100 years later they wheeled the now old traveller to the spot he claimed to have seen the miraculous future, they waited for his younger self to appear. When he didn't, they all looked at him. "I lied," he said.

In the 1990's Ray Bradbury did a half dozen book signings at my store, Celebrity Books, becoming our own resident author and signing thousands of books over the years. As I got to know him, I often remarked to others how Ray seemed to be a man who was reaping the rewards of doing what he loved.

❌ 1907 South Caliente Road
LARRY GELBART

Comedic scriptwriter of *MASH, Oh God, Tootsie* and more, owned this home in 1997. It was built in 1957 with 3 bedrooms and 2 baths, 2,287sf on a 4,356sf lot. Gelbart also produced 12 shows: *The Marty Feldman Comedy Machine*(1971-72), all 72 episodes of *MASH, Fast Track*(97-98), and more.

Ⓨ 1840 South Caliente Road
IRVING ALLEN

Producer would have been the partner of James Bond producer Albert R. Broccoli, but he dissolved the partnership too soon and lost out on the secret agent franchise. Allen bought this 3 bed 2 bath 1,600sf home brand new in 1957. It sits on a 10,890sf lot.

Z **2352 South Calle Palo Fierro**

HARRY CARAY

TV, radio and live broadcaster-announcer lived in this home with his wife Dolores till his death in 1998. Dolores still owns it. Caray broadcasted for the St. Louis Cardinals & Browns(1945-69), one year with the Oakland Athletics, the Cicago White Sox(1971-80) and then joined the Chicago Cubs(1981-87).

AA **2622 South Calle Palo Fierro**

DAVE CHASEN

Owner of Chasen's restaurant in Beverly Hills owned this home with his wife Maude Martin. Dave died in 1973. Maude lived on here till 1997. The home was sold from the family's estate in 1999. Chasen is credited with inventing the Shirley Temple non-alcoholic drink so the child star could enjoy the bar.

AB 2672 South Calle Palo Fierro
FRED "THE HAMMER" WILLIAMSON

Football player/actor/producer/director has lived in this home with his wife Linda since at least 1997. Williamson played football for the San Fran 49'ers (where he earned his nickname), the Pittsburg Steelers, Oakland Raiders, & K.C. Chiefs; all in the 1960's. He then switched to movies: acted in 113 films, directed 21, produced 17 and wrote 11.

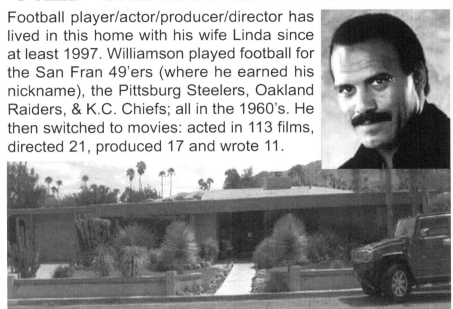

AC 2240 South Calle Palo Fierro #12
BERYL DAVIS

Big band singer lived here from 1992-2003. The 1,321sf condo was built in 1964. It has 2 bedrooms and 2 baths. Davis was discovered in London by Glenn Miller and sang with the Army Air Force Orchsetra during WWII. After, she sang for Sinatra & more.

327

AD 2080 South Camino Real

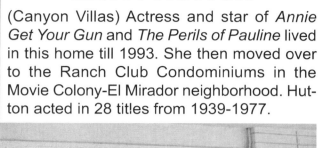

BETTY HUTTON

(Canyon Villas) Actress and star of *Annie Get Your Gun* and *The Perils of Pauline* lived in this home till 1993. She then moved over to the Ranch Club Condominiums in the Movie Colony-El Mirador neighborhood. Hutton acted in 28 titles from 1939-1977.

AE 2548 South Camino Real

DON ADAMS

Get Smart actor bought this 1962 3 bed 2 bath home in 1977. It has 2,504sf on a 10,454sf lot. Adams played in 34 titles from 1963-200, but once he played agent Maxwell Smart on *Get Smart*(1965-70) the role would forever over shadow his career. He reprised the role on the big screen, TV, movies, more.

AF 2585 South Camino Real

CHUCK CONNORS

Tall actor bought this 4 bed 3 bath home brand new and lived in it from 1963-1972. It has 2,473sf on a 10,890sf lot. Connors is best known for his role as Lucas McCain in the TV series *The Rifleman*(1958-63). He acted in 142 projects from 1942-2001, including: *Adventures of Superman*(1955), *Rod Serling's Night Gallery*(1972), & more.

AG 2617 South Camino Real

SIDNEY LANFIELD

Director/writer lived here with his actress wife Shirley Mason until he died in 1972. The 3 bed 3 bath 1964 home has 2,431sf on a 8,276sf lot. Lanfield wrote 11 screenplays during his 1926-67 career and directed 66 projects: *Wagon Train*('57-58), *McHale's Navy*('62-66) & *The Addams Family*('64-66).

AH **2688 South Camino Real**

WALT DISNEY

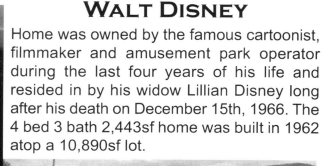

Home was owned by the famous cartoonist, filmmaker and amusement park operator during the last four years of his life and resided in by his widow Lillian Disney long after his death on December 15th, 1966. The 4 bed 3 bath 2,443sf home was built in 1962 atop a 10,890sf lot.

AI **2744 South Camino Real**

WILLIAM BENDIX

Actor lived here for one year in 1963. The 1962 home has 3,522sf of interior space with 3 bdrm and 3 bath on a 12,632sf lot. Bendix performed in 88 titles from 1942-65 including: *The Life of Riley*(1949), *Blackbeard, The Pirate*(1952), *Overland Trail*(1960), *Young Fury*(1965) and many more.

AJ 2195 South La Paz Way

ELEANOR PARKER

Actress and three time Oscar nominee has lived here since 1977. The 2,600sf condo was built in 1973. It has 3 bedrooms and 3 baths and sits on a 3,485sf lot. Parker played in 78 shows from 1941-91, and is best known for: *Caged*(1950), *Detective Story*(1951), *The Man With the Golden Arm*(1955) and *The Sound of Music*(1965).

AK 1508 South La Verne Way

LITA BARON

Actress and ex-wife of Rory Calhoun bought this 3 bed 4 bath condo new in 1976. it has 2,690sf on a 4,792sf lot. Baron acted in 25 titles from 1945-79, including: *Pan-Americana*(1945), *The I Love Lucy Show*(Cuban Pals 1952), *Death Valley Days*(1968-69).

AL **1642 South La Verne Way**

SHECKY GREEN

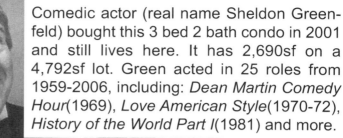

Comedic actor (real name Sheldon Green-feld) bought this 3 bed 2 bath condo in 2001 and still lives here. It has 2,690sf on a 4,792sf lot. Green acted in 25 roles from 1959-2006, including: *Dean Martin Comedy Hour*(1969), *Love American Style*(1970-72), *History of the World Part I*(1981) and more.

AM **2347 South Madrona Drive**

HUGO MONTENEGRO

Composer died here in 1981. It's a large 2 bed 3 bath condo with 2,552sf on a 3,920sf lot, built in 1972. Montenegro was an established musician when he began working for RCA records (1960's) & quickly moved to making soundtracks for Hollywood: *I Dream of Jeannie*, Clint Eastwood westerns, etc.

(AN) 2333 South Via Lazo

HARPER GOFF

Art Director moved here in 1978, where he lived till his death in 1993. The 1963 home has 3 bdrm 3 bath in 2,300sf on a 10,890sf lot. Goff worked on *Captain Blood*(1935) *20,000 Leagues Under the Sea*(1954), acted in *Dragnet*(1953-54), & did art for *Willy Wonka & the Chocolate Factory*(1971).

(AO) 1910 South Toledo Avenue

KEVIN COGAN

Formula One racing car driver grew up in this 3 bed 2 bath 1966 home while attending Palm Springs High School in 1972. It has 1,866sf and a 10,019sf lot. Cogan crashed in 1982 at the Indianapolis 500, won at Phoenix in 1986, crashed again in 1989 and 1991 at the Indy 500, then retired in 1993.

AP 2272 South Toledo Avenue

CHARLES LEMAIRE

Costume designer for 20th Century Fox, who won 3 Oscars and worked on 275 films, lived here till his death in PS in 1985. The 1972 4 bed 4 bath home has 3,515sf on a 12,197sf lot. Le Maire's Academy Awards were for: *All About Eve*(1950), *The Robe*(1953) and *Love is a Many Splendored Thing*(1955).

AQ 2514 South Toledo Avenue

FESS PARKER

Actor who portrayed Davy Crockett on *Disney's Wonderful World of Color*(54-56) and TV's *Daniel Boone*('64-70) lived in this 1974 home till 1990 with 2,097sf of living space, 2 bdrm 3 bath atop a 20,473sf lot. After retiring, Parker ran the Fess Parker Family Winery and Vineyards in Los Olivos, CA.

1578 Toledo Circle

MACK DAVID

In 1976, songwriter lived in this 1973 condo with 2,600sf and 3 bdrm 3 bath. David composed lyrics and music for 23 different TV shows and films and was nominated for 8 Oscars for Bibbidy-Bibbidy-Boo for *Cinderella* and more.

 ## 2220 Yosemite Drive

DAVID JANSSEN

Actor best known for his portrayal of Dr. Kimble on TV's The Fugitive purchased this 3 bed 3 bath home in 1967. It was built in 1965 with 3,314sf on a 16,553sf lot. Janssen played in 97 titles from 1945-81, including several of the *Francis the Talking Mule* movies and more.

KEELY SMITH

Singer bought this home in 1997. Smith is a long-time Las Vegas entertainer who performed on movie soundtracks from 1958-2010. Sinatra gave her away at her 1975 wedding.

AT 2250 Yosemite Drive

RICHARD KRISHER

Actor who had a two year run in 1967-68 in bit parts and then became a Palm Springs realtor, owned this 3,169sf 1968 home from 1996-2000, when he died in PS. Krisher got roles on 7 projects, including: playing a desk clerk on *The St. Valentine's Day Massacre*('67), a motorcycle cop on TV's *Batman*('67), *Lost in Space*('67), *The Detective*('68) & *The Boston Strangler*('68).

AU 2290 Yosemite Drive

WILLIAM DEMAREST

Actor who played Uncle Charley in *My Three Sons*(1960) lived in this 3 bed 3 bath home with his wife, Lucille Thayer, till his death in 1983. She owned it till 1997. It has 2,848sf on a 13,504sf lot. Demarest played in 168 projects from 1926-78, including: *Mr. Smith Goes to Washington*('39), *Twilight Zone*('64), more.

(AV) 1983 Yucca Place

BEVERLY WILLS

Actress and daughter of Joan Davis who died in a fire in this home on October 24, 1963. It was built in 1958 with 3 bdrm 2 bath 2,136sf on a 10,019sf lot. Wills played in 22 shows from 1938-64, including: *I Married Joan*('53-54), *Son of Flubber*('63), *Petticoat Junction*('63), *Mr. Ed*('63) and more.

Eric G. Meeks Colllection

Aerial photo of The Smoke Tree Ranch in the 1950's. The large undeveloped vacant stretch of land to the right will become the Canyon Country Club

Eric G. Meeks Colllection

Andreas Hills offers one of the most picturesque spots in Palm Springs, at the top of Andreas Hills Drive, if your looking for a great scenic view, want a special place to steal a kiss, go hiking, or looking for a thrilling bicycle ride.

Andreas Hills

The closest thing a person can own to sacred Indian land in Palm Springs is Andreas Hills. Only you can't own this tribal land. You have to lease it. With it's secluded eastern location in Palm Canyon, many of these homes and condos posess superior views of Mount San Jacinto and the city below; especially the original Andreas Hills condominiums that were constructed in 1970.

Since then, the area has become increasingly popular with residents who want to build a grand estate where they can enjoy the quiet serenity and natural surroundings the very south end of Palm Springs has to offer.

Large homes, many of them with 5,000sf+ sit on lots of 20,000sf or more. Some of the reasons this area has grown in popularity is because of the access to the nearly unlimited hiking trails into the Indian Canyons even further south and east and into the foothills of San jacinto to the west. One of these trails will deliver you into the back yard of Bob Hope's palatial Southridge estate only to be chased away by the ever present security guards. But, that doesn't stop folks from going there.

While you have your camera ready in Andreas Hills, you'll get a few celebrity homes shots to be sure, but you'll also want to snap a few pictures of of the beautiful scenery overlooking the south end of town. The picture on the left side of this page is my testimonial to one I have always found truly enticing.

The Indians have known of the beauty of this canyon for centuries. Many of the tribal members still live in the canyon named for one of the oldest Indian families in Palm Springs.

Andreas Hills

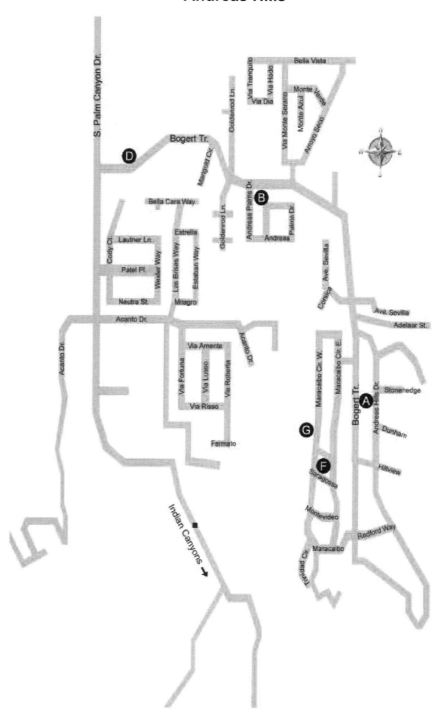

Ⓐ 3415 Andreas Hills Drive
GEORGE ENGLUND

Actor-writer-producer-director has lived in this home since 1997. It was built in 1970 with 2 bedrooms and 3 baths in 2,770sf. Englund starred in an episode of TV's *Lghts Out*. But he quickly switched to the production side of the camera, producing 13 projects including: *The Ugly American*(1959) starring his long-time friend Marlon Brando. More recently, he was a post-production executive on TV's *The Golden Girls*(1991-92)

Ⓑ 1034 Andreas Palms Drive
ANDREW NEIDERMAN

Author and his wife, Diane, moved to this 3 bed 4 bath 3,815sf home in 2002. It was built in 1990 and sits on a 23,958sf lot. Neiderman became the ghostwriter for the V.C Andrews Flowers in the Attic series after her death in 1986. He's written 43 novels since 1967, including The Devil's Advocate(1990).

Ⓓ 300 Bogert Trail

JOHN SCHLESINGER

Film director who made *Midnight Cowboy, The Day of the Locust, Marathon Man, The Falcon and the Snowman*, more, moved here in 2000 until he died in Palm Springs in 2003. The home, built in 1996, is 3,538sf with 3 bedrooms and 4 baths on a 21,344sf lot.

Ⓕ 64-894 Saragossa Drive

ANDREW NEIDERMAN

(Park Andreas) The first Palm Springs home of the author of The Devil's Advocate and the ghostwriter of many later V.C Andrews (posthumous) novels lived here. He is also the owner of Palm Springs Brewery Company. It was built in 1989 with 3 bedrooms 4 baths, 3,748sf of living space and a pool.

Ⓖ 38-430 West Maracaibo Road

MARIA RIVA

Daughter of Marlene Dietrich bought this 1988 home in 1990. It has 3,800sf with 2 bedrooms and 3 baths on a 19,166sf lot. Riva has acted in 24 projects from 1934-88, inlcuding the Bill Murray comedy Scrooged. She also wrote the 1992 biography of her mother.

```
DESERT  INN  THE  153 N Palm Cnyn Dr. P Spgs 2261
        (See Advertisement This Classification)
DOLL  HOUSE  THE
     1032 N Palm Cnyn Dr............P Spgs 7201
DON THE BEACHCOMBER CAFE
     120 Via Lola....................P Spgs 2061
DUNES  RESTAURANT
     238 N Palm Cnyn Dr............P Spgs 9014
El Jacal 67-778 Hwy 111 TrmvwVlg..P Spgs 8-8344
        (See Advertisement This Classification)
Farmhouse Restaurant
     68-981 Bdway CathdrlCty .......P Spgs 8-7372
Fireplace The 285 N Palm Cnyn Dr...P Spgs 5426
Flame Restaurant The                o
     391 S Palm Cnyn Dr............P Spgs 5168
Ham & Eggery The
     370 N Palm Cnyn Dr............P Spgs 4565
HOWARD MANOR 572 N Indian Av....P Spgs 2227
        (See Advertisement This Classification)
```

From the 1956 PS Phone Directory. Dunes owner, Irwin Rubenstein, never ran a display advertisement the entire time he owned the restaurant downtown Palm Springs..

Eric G. Meeks Colllection

Dean Martin playing golf at
Thunderbird Country Club in the 1960's.

Paul Pospesil Colllection

This photo of Cary Grant was taken about 1960 back in the
Andreas Hills area. Notice how impeccably dressed he is. His
Levi's are ironed crisp and he's sporting cuff links.

Eric G. Meeks Colllection

Araby below and Southridge above.

Araby, Los Compadres & Southridge

We'll attack three distinct neighborhoods at once in this chapter.

Araby: This neighborhood is broken into two parts itself these days; Araby Commons and Araby Cove and it makes sense. Commons is an assortment of homes and condos largely of the newer category, though are a few larger pioneer type properties. The Cove is almost all early Palm SPrings estates built in the shadow of the illustrious Southridge mountaintop devlopment. The Cove is also home to one fo Palm Springs urban legends: Munchkinville.

Los Compadres: Here we have a large section of nicely developed single family residences centered around one of the oldest riding stables still in existence. Almost all of the properties are on Indian lease land.

Southridge: The most exclusive of the celebrity neighborhoods in Palm Springs will not let you beyond its armed and guarded hillside gate. Once, as a young man, I ventured up to the gatehouse just to see what could be seen. The guard told me I wasn't even allowed to flip my car around the gatehouse. I had to back up and stay off property. He kept his hand on the butt of his revolver the entire time he spoke to me.

Here you'll find the Palm Springs celebrity elite. People who go beyond A-list and enter the realm of Hollywood royalty and the mega-moguls of American and international business circles. There's even one home where a James Bond movie was filmed.

Southridge can only be viewed from a distance.

Araby, Los Compadres & Southridge

Ⓐ 2630 Anza Trail

GRACE VANDERBILT

This is the home of a local nurse and not the daughter of Cornelius Vanderbilt III, nor the cousin to fashion designer Gloria Vanderbilt. This home is often confused with the heir to the Vanderbilt fortune. But she is merely a local hero of sorts in her own right; one who takes care of the sick and ailing and nurses them back to health. The home is now gone, the site an empty lot.

Ⓑ 2714 Anza Trail

ERLE STANLEY GARDNER

in 1956, the creator of *Perry Mason* lived in this 1,564sf 2 bed 2 bath 1946 home on a 33,106sf lot. Gardner published his first story in detective pulp magazines in 1923. But before his death in 1970, he'd written more than 80 Mason stories. The TV series *Perry Mason*('57-63) starred Raymond Burr.

Ⓒ 2742 Jacaranda Road

JOHN-PAUL RIVA

Grandson to Marlene Dietrich lived here with actress/wife Marilee Warner from 1995-2005. It's a newer home, built in 1993 with 3 bedrooms and 3 baths in 3,263sf of living space on a 16,988sf lot.

Ⓓ 1112 San Joaquin Drive

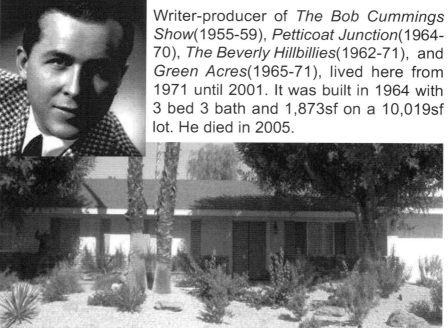

PAUL HENNING

Writer-producer of *The Bob Cummings Show*(1955-59), *Petticoat Junction*(1964-70), *The Beverly Hillbillies*(1962-71), and *Green Acres*(1965-71), lived here from 1971 until 2001. It was built in 1964 with 3 bed 3 bath and 1,873sf on a 10,019sf lot. He died in 2005.

Ⓔ 1807 Sandcliff Road

GORDON AYRES

I has been rumored that vintage Hollywood glamour photographer, Gordon Ayres, lived in this 1,569sf, bed 2 bath, 1964 condo. But it isn't true. The Ayres who lived here was simply a man with a similar name, who moved out in 1990.

Ⓕ 1861 Sandcliff Road

BENNIE LANE

(Garden Villas) Director of Make-up for Columbia Pictures, Screen Gems and Warner Brothers from 1955-1980 retired here in 1982. His credits include *Scaramouche*(1952) and *Vertigo*(1958). The 2 bed 2 bath 1,603sf condo was built in 1964.

Ⓖ 2390 South Araby Drive
SCOTT HOLDEN

The youngest son of actor William Holden lived here until 1993. The 2,202sf 3 bedroom 3 bath home sold for $1.8mil in 2007 and sits on a 16,117sf lot.

Ⓗ 1990 South Barona Road
WILLIAM S. DARLING

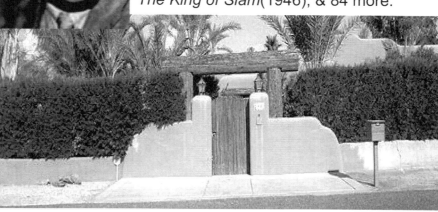

Three time Oscar winning set decorator & art director lived here for twenty years before his death in 1964. The home was built in 1938 with 2 bedrooms and 3 baths, a total of 2,562sf on a 21,344sf site. His credits include: *Poor Little Rich Girl*(1936), *Anna & The King of Siam*(1946), & 84 more.

❶ 2088 South Barona Road
NICOLAI REMISOFF

Art director and production designer retired to this 1940 2 bed 2 bath 1,547sf home in 1965 and lived here for ten years till his death. Remisoff worked on 43 projects, including: *Of Mice and Men*('39), TV's *Gunsmoke*('55-57) & *Ocean's Eleven*('60), more.

❶ 2175 Southridge Drive
ARTHUR ELROD

Built in 1968 and designed by LA architect John Lautner, this 7,366sf 2 bed 3 bath home was first owned by Interior Designer Elrod. Home was the site for James Bond enemy Blofeld's desert fortress in 1971's *Diamonds Are Forever*.

RON BURKEL

Food-4-Less Supermarkets Vice-President was the second owner of this home. He bought it for $1.3mil in September, 1995.

Ⓚ 2203 Southridge Drive

EDWIN H. MORRIS

World's largest music publisher, built this 4 bed 4 bath 4,493sf home in 1964. It was designed by architect Hugh Kapur. Morris first began publishing music for Warner Brothers in 1927. But in 1941 branched out on his own becoming the premiere publisher of Hollywood and Broadway soundtracks.

STEVE MCQUEEN & ALI MACGRAW

McQueen lived here first with wife Neile Adams in 1969-1972 and then later with Ali MacGraw till 1976. He would dune buggy up the mountain to his Southridge address even though his neighbors frowned on it. The tracks are still visible climbing up the hill behind the BMW dealer.

During this period of McQueens life he was known to use marijuana and cocaine while still maintaining a 2 hour a day workout regimen. He also completed the films: *The Getaway, Papillon, Towering Inferno*, more. MacGraw claimed in her autobiography, Moving Pictures, to be an alcohol and sex addict. The two were mistakenly refused entry to the Grand Opening party of Melvyn's Restaurant at the Ingleside Inn while looking too rough and showing up on a motorcycle. They divorced in 1978.

354

Ⓛ 2379 Southridge Drive

JOHN H. JOHNSON

Jet magazine founder/publisher and his wife Eunice owned this 5 bed 7 bath home from 1974-2011. The 5,356sf home was built in 1964 and the pool is built on a jutting outcropping of rock, virtually hanging above a cliff. Linda Johnson Rice, daughter and now President of Jet, currently owns the home.

Ⓜ 2399 Southridge Drive

EDWARD GIDDINGS

Architect Giddings designed this home called "La Piedra" (House of Stone) with 5 bedrooms 6 baths and 5,100sf in 1983. It has granite walls, a putting green, a pool, a shuffleboard court, and a tennis court, on a 98,010sf lot.

N 2433 Southridge Drive

WILLIAM HOLDEN

Holden was a natural leading man by only his 5th film. He was in 74 total.

The actor bought the land in 1972. He first hired E. Stewart Williams to design the home but thought it too pricey and then hired Hugh Kaptur for a more streamlined house, which he built in 1977. The home is 6,657sf with 3 bedrooms 4 baths on a 161,608sf lot with a pool.

Holden moved to this Southridge home in 1977, at the age of 59, a year after the release of his film *Network* and while still working on *Damien: Omen II*. At the time, he was dating Stefanie Powers and enjoyed a wild life of motorcycles, art and a pet python named Bertie. The couple would ride both dirt bikes on the desert floor or ride tandem on Holden's 1000cc street bike.

He had four more films before his untimely demise. But none of them were blockbusters compared to his projects of old. Finally, in November, 1981, he suffered a fatal fall while drinking in his Santa Monica beach front home, resulting in a cut to the head from his coffee table. He bled to death.

◉ 2466 Southridge Drive

BOB & DOLORES HOPE

"The House of Hope" was completed in 1979. It burnt to the steel girder frame in 1973. Designed by architect John Lautner, home is also known as "The Flying Saucer." Hope owned this home from its inception to his death. It is still owned by the Dolores Hope Trust. It is a massive 17,531sf with 6 bedrooms and 12 baths on a 138,085sf lot.

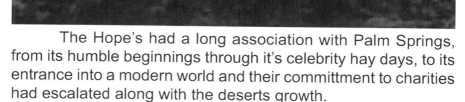

The Hope's had a long association with Palm Springs, from its humble beginnings through it's celebrity hay days, to its entrance into a modern world and their committment to charities had escalated along with the deserts growth.

The home was used primarily for parties and gala functions of the Bob Hope Golf Classic and the Bob Hope Cultural Center.

in the final years of Bob's life (1903-2003), he rekindled a love for the simple pleasures of Palm Springs and a few times a year someone would rush into my store, Celebrity Books, saying, "Do you have any books or photos of Bob Hope? He's down at the ice cream shop right now and I want to get it signed!"

DID WIZARD OF OZ MIDGETS SETTLE IN OLD PALM SPRINGS?

Eric G. Meeks Colllection

Shown here is the main home of the four structures which make up the Munchkinville neighborhood. To see the homes, take South Araby Drive to the very top of the road, just before it is barricaded with a large metal gate blocking the road, and look down the remaining dirt road to your right.

Ⓟ @2560 South Araby Drive
MUNCHKINVILLE
A PALM SPRINGS URBAN LEGEND

Munchkinville, Munchkin Land, Midgetville, Midget Town: All are names of a mythical place I'd heard about since I was a child in the 1970's.

As the legend goes, after the Wizard of Oz was made back in the 1930's some of the midget actors took their earnings and bought this land in the Araby area. They played a key role in the building of these four homes; wanting door ways, windows, counters and roof lines to be built especially to size for the little people. Most of the houses were made out of natural rock and they were constructed at the end of a long dead end street out of sight from the rest of the world. They wanted to create a place for themselves in the celebrity haven of Palm Springs.

Fast forward 30+ years, to just recently actually, and I found myself in Palm Springs one day with a digital camera in my hand and more time than I'd scheduled for. I drove around the neighborhood, to the top of Araby Drive and found a small wide spot in the road with signs that read: NO PARKING ANYTIME. I parked. Ahead of me was an old water tower, and beneath it was an iron cross bar blocking access from Araby Drive onto a much older and narrower dirt road now overgrown with weeds and brush. It descended as it wound around the base of the mountain, staying just above the wash below till it reached a small cluster of homes, made of stone. They were hardly discernible, blending into the mountain and desert so natural and covered in decades of plant growth. I didn't walk down. They looked as if they hadn't been lived in for years.

I knew I'd found it, so I posted my thoughts on Facebook to all my old lifelong friends. There were some 50+ comments posted in return. Seems everyone had a story to tell about Munchkinville. Some believed they had found it when they were young. Others claimed it a false rumor.

But, all knew of the legend.

Seven Lakes

This prestigious Country Club seems, for reasons unbeknownst to the author, to have become the celebrity home to former wives and divorcees. Or at least a higher concentration of them vis-a-vis more typical celebrities.

I doubt this was the intention of developer Johnny Dawson, who, in the 1950's, turned a ten year lucarative professional golf career into a launching pad for golf course design. Before committing to Seven Lakes as his golf and architectural Grand Opus, Dawson designed and built the courses for Thunderbird Country Club, El Dorado and the La Quinta Resort.

In 1962, when deciding on the modernistic style of the clubhouse and buildings, he hired architect William F. Cody, who had already designed The Spa Hotel, Saint Teresa Catholic Church, L'Horizon Hotel and soon to come: Sunrise Plaza and Palm Springs Public Library. Seven Lakes is a community of some 350 condos. The first of which were completed in 1964 on a private executive level golf course

Dwight Eisenhower is credited with a hole in one from the thirteenth tee in 1968, only one year before his death at 78. Ike had a long history in the desert and is said to have written his memoirs while living at Indian Palms Country Club in indio.

Dawsons wife, Velma, had her own claim to fame. It was she who created the original Howdy Doody doll, whose freckle-faced shenanigans kept a generation of kids enthralled to his daily childrens' western entertainment hour in the 1950's. Velma was only paid $300 for the famous red-headed marionette and there were three dolls created in all. One now resides in the Detroit institute of Arts, one is in the Smithsonian, and, in 1997, one sold to a private collector for $113,000.

Seven Lakes

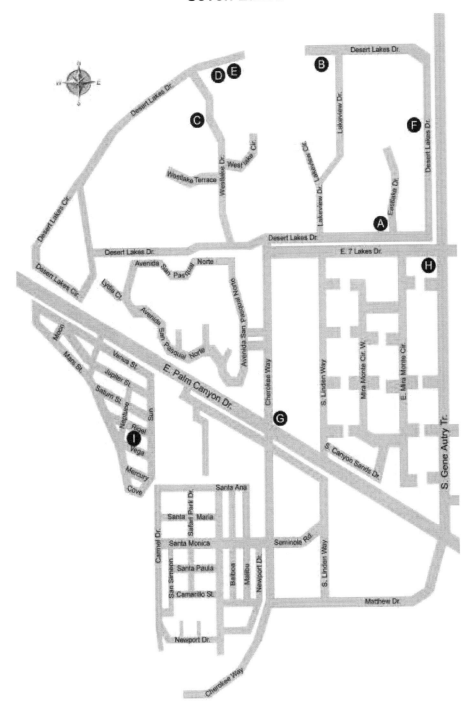

Ⓐ 12 Desert Lakes Drive

JOHNNY DAWSON

Retired golfer turned designer & builder of Seven Lakes Country Club lived here within his own development in 1966. His particular condo was built in 1972 and is a large 2 bed 2 bath with 1,555sf of interior space. He also designed courses for Thunderbird, El Dorado and La Quinta.

Ⓑ 168 Desert Lakes Drive

DON WILSON

Radio announcer and actor lived here in 1977. It has 1,965sf 2 bedrooms 2 baths & a fairway view. Wilson played in several shows from the 1930's to 40's. But he's best known as a supporting actor on episodes of *The Jack Benny Program*.

Ⓒ 171 Desert Lakes Drive

BRENDA MARSHALL

Actress was William Holden's ex-wife who, after thirty years of marriage, divorced him in 1971 and she lived here from 1973 till her death in PS in 1992. This 2 bed 2 bath 2,741sf fairway condo was built in 1967. Her real name was Ardis Ankerson.

Ⓓ 193 Desert Lakes Drive

HARRY GERSTAD

Two-time Oscar winning film editor whose work included *Death of A Salesman*(1951), *The Adventures of Superman*(1953-57) and *Walking Tall*(1973) and then retired to this 2 bed 2 bath 1967 condo with 1,599sf.. He edited 39 projects from 1945-75. He died in Palm Springs in 2002 at 93 years old.

E ## 195 Desert Lakes Drive

CARMENE ENNIS

Singer and former wife of orchestra leader Skinnay Ennis has lived here since 1975. Skinnay got his first break in college. in the 1920's, when he became a drummer for Hal Kemp. Later, he joined the *Bob Hope Radio Show*, while touring in the off season and then, after WWII, the *Abbott & Costello Radio Show*. He choked on a bone in a Beverly Hills restaurant in 1963.

F ## 300 Desert lakes Drive

LUCILLE DEMAREST

Wife of actor who was best known for playing Uncle Charley in *My Three Sons* moved to this 3 bed 3 bath 2,114sf condo in 1997. It was sold in 2004. William Demarest played in 168 titles between 1926 and 1978, including: *The Jazz Singer*(1927), *Charlie Chan at the Opera*(1936), *Mr. Smith Goes To washington*(1939), *Alfred Hitchcock Presents*(1958), *Twilight Zone*('64).

Ⓖ 4200 East Palm Canyon Drive

GENE AUTRY HOTEL & THE PARKER

Formerly the Holiday Inn. Bought by Autry in 1961 and he originally called it the Melody Ranch. Shortly after buying it though, he renamed it the Gene Autry Hotel. Besides being a favorite hangout for Autry's celebrity friends, the California Angels used to stay here up until the 1980's when Palm Springs was still the baseball team's home field for Spring and Summer training. Autry sold the hotel in 1994 to Merv Griffin on a Warranty Deed and the property was remodeled and renamed Merv Griffin's Resort & Givenchy Spa. Under Griffins ownership many celebrities and social elite stayed there. But it's most famous guest was Robert Downey, Jr.(35 then), who, while on leave from the *Ally McBeal* set, stayed in room 311 when he was busted for drugs with a prostitute dressed in a Superman outfit on November 25, 2000, just one day after Thanksgiving. Then in 1998 it sold again, and again in 2002. These days it's simply called The Parker.

From the 1968 Palm Springs Phone Directory.

Ⓗ 2277 South Gene Autry Trail #D

ROBERT KLINE

(Canyon Sands) Not the comedian, but the producer of 55 titles, mostly documentaries and TV movies, including: Assassinations: An American Nightmare(1975), The Vietnam Experience(1989), Harley Davidson: The Spirit of America(2005), The Sandman(2011), Afganistan & Beyond(2012), & more, lived here from 2003-2005. It's a 2 bed 2 bath 1977 condo with 1,404sf.

Ⓘ 186 Vega Street

LILLIAN ROTH

(Horizon Mobile Home Village) Broadway & film actress, singer, lived here in 1970. Roth made her Broadway debut at 6 years old in 1916 then went on to act in 23 titles from 1929-79 including: Animal Crackers(1930), The Red Skelton Hour(1954), and more.

Paul Pospesil Colllection

Harpo Marx goofing around with a golfing friend at the
La Quinta Resort in the 1960's.

Eric G. Meeks Colllection

Taken from Golf Club Drive looking west over the 18th, 10th, 1st and 9th fairways of the Old Course at Tahquitz Creek Golf Course.

Golf Club Estates

In this chapter we have two distinct neghborhoods rolled into one: The Golf Club Estates and the Golf Club Drive Condos.

The Golf Club Estates were built by father and son developer team, George and Robert Alexander, beginning in 1961. Now it's called the Tahquitz Creek Estates, but at its inception there was no Tahquitz Creek Golf Course. These homes are an example of the Alexander's best quality of work. Good sized homes of 1,500sf-2,200sf sit on lots facing the city's owned and operated Old Course. This is the neighborhood where i grew up and what I find interesting is back in my youth, of the 1970's, these were simply the homes everybody lived and grew up; not the desireable trendy area its become today.

The Golf Club Drive condominiums of Mountain Shadows, Fairways, Los Pueblos, and Villas de Las Flores(formerly called New Horizons) were constructed but a decade later in the early 1970's. These condos take advantage of a unique situation. They get to enjoy the benefits of a golf course comunity without having to pay the association fees that usually go along with it, due to the fact that the City of Palm Springs maintains the Tahquitz Creek Golf Course around their perimieter.

Because of the time period of the development in this area it is the least populated with celebrities and is therefore rightfully included at the end of the book. But I do recall from my youth, while delivering Desert Sun newspapers - when such a youthful employment was common place - that one day in New Horizons condominiums (now called Villas de las Flores) I came across actress Kristy McNichols, of TV drama show *Family* fame, lounging by a pool.

Golf Club Estates

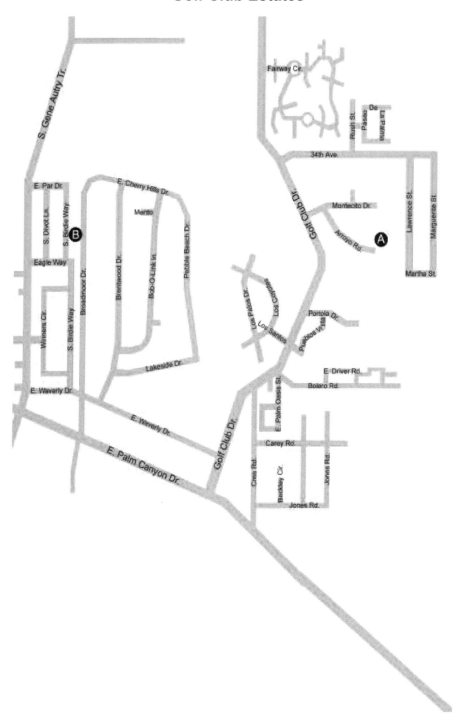

Ⓐ 6176 Arroyo Road
JO SWERLING, JR.

(Mountain Shadows condominiums) TV producer of *Baretta*('75), *The A-Team*('83-87), *21 Jump Street*('87-91), more, lived here in 1981. Swerling began producing shows with *Kraft Suspense Theatre*('67). His works also include: *The Rockford Files*('74-75), & *Simon and Simon*('83).

Ⓑ 2047 Broadmoor Drive
ERIC G. MEEKS

Former home of author Eric G. Meeks, where he lived during his youth with his parents Darrell and Shirley Meeks from 1978-1987 in this 3 bed 2 bath Alexander home. His parents owned it till 2000. His books include: Witch of Tahquitz, PS I Love Lucy, Author Murders, and more.

Palm Springs HIstorical Society

Betty Ford welcoming Frank Sinatra with a kiss to a
Betty Ford Recovery Center fundraiser in 1977.

Down Valley Addresses

The transforming of Thunderbird Dude Ranch in the 1950's started down valley growth. Desi Arnaz's Western Hills resort in indian Wells expanded it, as did the construction of College of the Desert in 1968. Even when I first moved here in 1976, Palm Canyon Drive was but a two lane blacktop road once you got out of Palm Springs and there were only three stoplights separating Sunrise Way in Palm Springs from Monterey Drive in Palm Desert. And by then, the Bob Hope Golf Classic (Chrysler was not involved yet) was drawing tens of thousand of visitors a year to view celebrities down valley.

in 1983, the Palm Desert Mall (now the Westfield Mall) was constructed and the demographical landscape of the desert was changed forever.

These days there's just as many celebrities and captains of industry spread out over the entire Coachella valley as the Golden Years of Palm Springs can claim during it's hey days.

I know there are more celebrities deserving to go in this section than I currently have to list. This is probably the number one area I can use some help with. So, if you know of any celebrities worthy of being added to this section of the book, please email me at MeeksEric@hotmail.com.

Thank you.

WALTER ANNENBERG
Sunnylands Estate, Rancho Mirage
At the corner of Frank Sinatra Drive and Bob Hope Drive.

Publishing magnate who took over his fathers business of publishing a racing form in the 1930's and grew it to outsanding porportion. He was the creator of TV Guide & Seventeen magazines and was married to Leonore Cohn (second marriage) in 1951. Richard Nixon appointed him Ambassador to the United Kingdom from 1969-74. After his Ambassadorship he was made an honorary Knight of the Order of the British Empire, was named an Officer of the French Legion of Honor, and was given a Presidential Medal of Freedom by Ronald Reagan, among other awards. in 1988, Annenberg sold most of his publishing empire to Rupert Murdoch to $3billion. He died in 2002.

DESI ARNAZ
Thunderbird Country Club, Rancho Mirage
71475 Mashie Drive/71475 Kaye Ballard Lane

Desi and his second wife Edith Hirsh bought this 1955 home in 1963. It has 3 bedrooms 2 baths in 2,094sf and a pool on a 9,583sf lot. He eventually sold it completely furnished to actress Kaye Ballard of the Desilu TV sitcom *Mother's-In-Law*(1967-69) fame and the street was renamed in her honor.

TAMMY FAYE BAKKER & ROE MESSNER
Lake Mirage, Rancho Mirage
72727 Country Club Drive

Tammy faye's second husband, married in 1993, after only divorcing Jim (in jail for fraud) one year earlier. Messner was the developer of The Heritage Park and PTL Church which the Bakkers lost due to Jim's attempt to bribe his mistress Jessica Hahn into silence and fraudulent management and financial tactics being discovered during a hostile takeover by rival televangelist Jerry Falwell. After the fall of PTL, Messner was the largest creditor at the bankruptcy trial, but eventually went to jail for fradulent claims himself during his own bankruptcy in 1996.

LUCILLE BALL & DESI ARNAZ
Thunderbird Country Club, Rancho Mirage
40241 Club View Drive

Built in 1955 and bought brand new by Lucy and Desi, this 5,705sf home was the primary address of Lucy and Desi in the desert. It is still owned by Mary Morton, the widow of Lucille Ball's second husband Gary Morton.

KAYE BALLARD
Thunderbird Country Club, Rancho Mirage
71475 Mashie Drive/71475 Kaye Ballard Lane

Actress from *The Mother-In-Laws* bought this home fully furnished from Desi in 1970. Address was changed to Kaye Ballard Lane. She still lives here.

JOHNNY & LAUREN BENCH
Mission Hills-Gary Player Course, Rancho Mirage
138 Royal Saint Georges Way

Cincinatti Reds baseball catcher and his wife have lived here since purchasing it in 2006 for $1,395,000. It's a 4 bed 5 bath 3,598sf home, built in 2004 on a 17,424sf lot with a pool and a fairway view.

CAROL CHANNING
Thunderbird Country Club, Rancho Mirage
4 Boothill Circle

Hello Dolly actress has owned this home since 2008. Prior to this home, she lived in Sunrise Country Club.

WILLIAM DEVANE
Thermal, CA
84393 61st Avenue

The actor has owned agricultural acreage - nearly 6 acres - with a 2 bed 2 bath 1,509sf home on it since at least 2006. He has also owned restaurants in Indio and La Quinta, now closed.

GERALD & BETTY FORD
Thunderbird Country Club, Rancho Mirage
40471 Sand Dune Road

Former President of the United Sates and philanthropic wife have owned this 6 bed 7 bath 6,316sf home for more than 30 years. Ford is best known as the President who pardoned Richard Nixon and served on the warren commission assigned to investigate the assassination of John F. Kennedy.He achieved Eagle Scout status at a young age and played football for the University of Michigan. Betty Ford is best known for founding the Betty Ford Center for substance abuse and addiction recovery, located at Eisenhower Hospital in Rancho Mirage. The Ford's did me a really nice favor in about 1995, by agreeing to autograph about 100 biographical books by Mrs. Ford (*The Times of My Life*) and 4 by President Ford (*A Time to Heal*). A year later, I was low on Christmas money and recontacted the Ford's, through their staff via the phone book, and Mrs. Ford bought the bulk of the remainder of myinventory of her book. It was out-of-print by then. So two Christmases were made by this deal: mine with the revenue from the sold books and Mrs. Fords., who now had about 75 signed books to give away as Christmas gifts.

BILL & MELINDA GATES
The Vintage, Indian Wells
46309 Jacaranda Road

Owner of Microsoft and his wife own this 3 bed 5 bath 5,903sf home, which was built in 1986. It sits on a 17,860sf lakeview lot.

PHILIP H. & PENELOPE KNIGHT
La Quinta, CA
77185 Avenida Arteaga

Founders of NIKE shoes have owned this 3 bed 4 bath 4,437sf home with a pool since 1998. Whenever they come to town they head straight to the Barnes & Noble where they feed their desire for massive amounts of literature and magazines.

TIM & BEVERLY LEHAYE
Desert Lakes CC, Rancho Mirage
899 Island Drive #704

Since 1993 the author of the Left Behind series and his wife have owned this 3 bed 4 bath 5,281sf condo, built in 1973.

GUY MADISON
Morongo Valley
50265 Aspen Road

Cowboy actor built this large western style ranch home on 10 acres before he died. Author Eric G. Meeks's parents, Darrell and Shirley Meeks bought it in 2000, dealing primarily with the deceased actors' daughter.

PETER MARSHALL
Palm Valley Country Club, Palm Desert
38029 Crocus Lane

Host of Hollywood Squares and his wife, Laurie, live in this 2 bed 3 bath 1,605sf condo.

RACHEL MCLISH & RON SAMUELS
Rancho Mirage
25 Judd Terrace

Female bodybuilder and her producer husband lived here in 1996.

OZZY & SHARON OSBOURNE
Thunderbird Cove, Rancho Mirage
71467 Country Club Drive

Lead singer of Black Sabbath and his X-factor Judge wife stayed here in 1986 while being an outpatient at the Betty Ford Center. I delivered a telegram to Ozzy at the time. Sharon answered the door and yelled back to Ozzy, who appeared at the end of the hall & mumbled incoherently, before Sharon took the telegram.

PATTI PAGE
Rancho Mirage
71537 Highway 111 #K

Singer used this address for her business address in 1996.

ARNOLD & WINIFRED PALMER
La Quinta
52123 Dunlevie Court

Golfer and his wife live in this 3 bed 3 bath 2,617sf home on a 16,988sf lot. They also own Arnold Palms restaurant.

ANTHONY ROBBINS
PGA West, La Quinta, CA
56525 Riviera

The motivational speaker and author, Robbins, who originally bought it with his first wife and she shared the deed with him (Rebecca, AKA Becky). She quitclaimed herself off the title in 2003 after their divorce. The home is a 3 bed 4 bath condo with 2,353sf and a six car garage, built in 1990. Robbins has owned it since at least 2000, but may have got it brand new or built it.

CHARLES "BUDDY" ROGERS
Rancho Mirage
8 Cromwell Cromwell Court

Actor and husband to Mary Pickford.

KURT RUSSELL & GOLDIE HAWN
Big Horn, Palm Desert
534 Mesquite Hills Drive

Actor Russell and actress Hawn have owned this 3 bedroom 5 bath 5,722sf 2001 home since 2003. it sits on a 48,352 western facing fairway view.

BARBARA SINATRA
The Vintage, Indian Wells
10 Windermere Court

Wife of Frank Sinatra has owned this 3 bed 3 bath 3,306sf condo since 2000.

FRANK SINATRA
Tamarisk Country Club, Rancho Mirage
70588 Frank Sinatra Drive

Two home compound of Sinatra's, complete with extra bungalows, railroad car pool house, movie theatre, large model train set room, and helicopter pad which the singer & actor owned from 1957-1995, until he sold it to Canadian Jimmy Pattison.

RICHARD BERNARD "RED" SKELTON
Tamarisk Country Club, Rancho Mirage
37801 Thompson Road

Till 1999, circus clown who made the jump to comedic acting and then later in life became a famous painter of clowns lived in this 3 bed 5 bath 3,528sf home on a 19,076sf lot. I cooked him dinner a couple of times when he came into the Chart House restaurant, where I was a broilerman/cook from 1980-87.

RALPH WAITE
Palm Desert
73317 Ironwood Street

Since 1992, the actor most famous for his role playing the dad of the Walton family in the 1970's TV show, *The Walton's*, has lived in this 2,542sf 4 bed 4 bath home on a 20,038sf lot. Mr. Waite invited me over once about 1997 to appraise and purchase a large portion of his personal library. He was a lover of Coachella Valley history and in particular the history of water rights. We made the deal and his collection became a part of my personal collection.

JOSEPH & DEE WAMBAUGH
Thunderbird Country Club, Rancho Mirage
41015 Rincon Road
Best-selling author and his wife owned this 4 bed 5 bath 6,747sf home on a 75,359sf lot till 2001.

PAUL ZASTUPNEVICH
Palm Desert
75179 La Sierra Drive
Costume designer and assistant to movie producer Irwin Allen lived here in 1996.

From the 1963 Palm Springs area phone book.

Paul Pospesil Colllection

Lucille Ball was the 1964 Palm Springs
Queen of the Desert Circus Parade.

Unverified Addresses

This chapter is a list of either properties of which:

1) I cannot honestly confirm the celebrity owned, rented nor even slept here.

or

2) I do know that the celebrity owns or has lived here in the desert, yet I have so far not been able to ascertain their actual address.

So, if you can give me any leads, rumors, innuendo, or solid facts of which I can further my knowledge in this regard, I wold be eternally grateful.

Please send all information to: MeeksEric@hotmail.com

Palm Springs Celebrity Homes

LUCILLE BALL & DESI ARNAZ
1194 North Via Miraleste, Palm Springs

RONA BARRETT
840 Las Palmas, Palm Springs

RALPH BELLAMY
187 San Marcos Way, Palm Springs

JACK BENNY
1700 North Via Norte, Palm Springs

CLARA BOW
184 Encanto, Palm Springs

RAY BRADBURY
1100 Murray Canyon, Palm springs

GEORGE BURNS & GRACIE ALLEN
987 North Avenida Palos Verdes, Palm Springs

FRANK CAPRA
La Quinta

CHARLIE CHAPLIN
Cahuilla, Palm Springs

NAT "KING" COLE
1258 North Rose Avenue, Palm Springs

JOAN CRAWFORD
Lugo/Corner of Belardo, Palm Springs

RAYMOND CREE
442 West Hermosa Place, Palm Springs

Unverified Addresses

BETTE DAVIS

784 Patencio, Palm Springs

SAMMY DAVIS, JR.

222 West Chino Drive, Palm Springs

SAMMY DAVIS, JR.

444 West Chino Drive, Palm Springs

HORACE DODGE

893 Abrigo Road, Palm Springs

DWIGHT EISENHOWER

Indio & Smoketree, Palm Springs

CHARLIE FARRELL

453 San Carlos Road, Palm Springs

ALICE FAYE

Thunderbird Ranch, Rancho Mirage

ANNETTE FUNICELLO

CLARK GABLE

Bermuda Dunes Country Club

CLARK GABLE & CAROLE LOMBARD

222 West Chino Canyon Drive, Palm Springs

ZSA ZSA GABOR

595 West Chino Canyon Road

GRETA GARBO

287 West Racquet Club Road

JANET GAYNOR

MERV GRIFFIN
La Quinta

HUGH HEFFNER
South Manzanita, Palm Springs

LEE IACOCCA

REGGIE JACKSON

HENRY KISSINGER
JACK LALANNE

HARPER LEE

JOHNNY LONGDEN

SHIRLEY MACLAINE

JOHN MCENROE
MARILYN MONROE
1326 North Rose Avenue, Palm Springs
& 358 East Via Alta Mira, Palm Springs
& 953 North Avenida Palmas, Palm Springs

JACK NICKLAUS

RICHARD NIXON

CHRISTINA ONASSIS
187 San Marcos Way, Palm Springs

ANNE RICE

GINGER ROGERS

KENNY ROGERS
555 North Patencio Road, Palm Springs

WILL ROGERS
Palm Springs

JOHN SANDFORD

RANDOLPH SCOTT
333 East Tamarisk, Palm Springs

DINAH SHORE
432 North Hermosa Drive, Palm Springs

BARBRA STREISAND & JAMES BROLIN
555 North Patencio Road, Palm Springs

ELIZABETH TAYLOR
Rancho Mirage

MARLO THOMAS
Ridge Road, Palm Springs

ROBERT WAGNER
Down Valley

JACK L. WARNER
1050 Cahuilla, Palm Springs

MICHELLE WIE

Special Thanks

This book could not have been possible if not for the help and support of the following people: First and foremost, my wife Tracey, who had to put up with me crawling out of bed more times than I can count at 4am to continue writing; my dad Darrell(deceased) who inspired me to create the *Facts & Legends of the Village of Palm Springs* series; Sally McManus, former President of the Palm Springs Historical Society; Reno and Laura Montana of the Elvis-Graceland West estate, Paul Pospesil for allowing me to purchase the rights to some of his fabulous photos; Barry Spencer for his editing assistance, Christian Kandora for resolving a QuarkExpress PDF export issue during the final publishing sequences, Bruce Sherman of Advantage Title for helping me verify some of the more difficult addresses, and the staff at the Palm Springs Public Library.

I also appreciate the moral support and helping moments of the people who helped me unravel some small knots in the histories uncovered herein: Sylvia Schmidt of Locations Unlimited (check out her shooting location website for unique desert film locations at http://www.locationunlimited.com); Robin and Heidi Simmons & Ron and Jennifer Klotchman for their constant emotional support at having taken on such a big project; Corey Yack for driving around with me at times to snap some of the celebrity homes pictures; and all my Facebook friends who gave little snippets of history that added such great first hand information and flavor to the celebrities stories.

And I don't want to forget my Mom, Shirley Meeks-Mahana, who permanently loaned me the cameras necessary for all the photos.

Thank you,
- EGM

Bibliography

Palm Springs Confidential, Howard Johns, Barricade Books, 2004.

Jack's Palm Springs and Valley Cities Close Up, Jack Titus, Prickly Pear Publishing, 2000.

Palm Springs First 100 Years, Mayor Frank M. Bogert, A Wenkham/Candere Book, Palm Springs HAssociates, Publisher, 1987.

Palm Springs Legends: Creation of a Desert Oasis, Greg Niemann, Sunbelt Books, 2006

Palm Springs Map of the Stars' Homes Self Guided Tour, Locations Unlimited, 2004

Palm Springs Celebrity Houses, @1997, a privately researched list I bought from someone who I can't remember back when I had my first bookstore on Tahquitz Canyon Drive.

Richards Celebrity Address List, Winter/Spring 1988

Palm Springs Phone Books 1944-1975, Courtesy of Palm Springs Public Library

Webliography

http://www.biography.com
http://www.cobbles.com
http://www.drummerworld.com
http://www.ibdb.com
http://www.imdb.com
http://www.findagrave.com
http://www.latimes.com
http://www.palmspringslife.com
http://www.palzoo.net
http://www.popstars.net
http://www.sydevore.com
http://www.wikipedia.org

Images Courtesy of

Associated Press International
DoctorMacro.com
Eric G. Meeks Personal Collection
Larry Edmonds Bookshop
Marlene4ever at the German language Wikipedia
MGM Studios
Palm Desert Historical Society
Palm Springs Historical Society
Paramount Studios
Paul Pospesil Collection
RKO Studios
United Artists
United Press international
Warner Brothers
Warner Bothers Animation

Index

Index

A

Don Adams 328
Eadie Adams 243
Al Adamson 172, 277
Buddy Adler 72
John Agar 148
Chris Alcaide 191
George Alexander 233, 239
Robert Alexander 77, 239
Gracie Allen 174, 385
Irving Allen 325
Gitta Alpar 219
Bob Anderson 192
Herbert Anderson 155
Kenneth Anger 178
Walter Annenberg 376
Colleen Applegate 37
Thomas Ardies 230
Arthur Arling 46
Russell Arms 54
Desi Arnaz 116, 180, 376, 377, 382, 385
George Arnold 112
Vivian Austin 58
Gene Autry 125, 366
Hy Averback 43
John Aylesworth 317
Gordon Ayres 351

B

Faye Bainter 300
Jim Bakker 167, 298
Tammy Faye Bakker-Messner 167, 298, 376
Lucille Ball 116, 180, 240, 377, 385
Kaye Ballard 377
Joseph Barbera 76
Don Barclay 65
Lita Baron 331
Rona Barrett 102
Gene Barry 313
Les Baxter 156
Irving Beecher 168
Dorothy Bekins 309
Ralph Bellamy 385
Johnny Bench 377
William Bendix 199, 330
Louis Benoist 281
Jack Benny 137, 166, 174, 385
Edward Bergen 101
Polly Bergen 198
Busby Berkeley 169
Pandro "Pan" Berman 297
Bruno Bernard 96, 209
Biltmore Hotel 256, 257
Claude Binyon 121
Mr. Blackwell 50
June Blanchard 302
Frank Bogert 67, 232, 240
Mary Bono 285
Sonny Bono 60, 278, 285, 299
Arthur K. Bourne 200
Clara Bow 141 385
Stephen Boyd 191
Ray Bradbury 324, 385
Harry Brand 160
Milton Bren 37
Samuel Briskin 38
Oscar Brodney 308
James Brolin 388
Harry Joe Brown 76

Robert Buckner 322
Zaddie Bunker 118
Paul Burke 53
Ron Burkel 353
George Burns 174, 385
Charles Butterworth 33

C

Sammy Cahn 100
Rory Calhoun 162
Camelot Theatre 231
Arthur Cameron 119
Milton Caniff 147
Judy Canova 180
Eddie Cantor 157
Truman Capote 158
Frank Capra 385
Harry Caray 326
Kitty Carlisle 133
Hoagy Carmichael 86
Regina Carrol 277
Sue Carroll 186
Jean Carson 323
Casa Blanca Motor Lodge 277
Don Castle 25
Nick Castle 181
Raymond Chandler 302
Carol Channing 377
Charlie Chaplin 385
Cyd Charisse 111
Leslie Charteris 223
Dave Chasen 326
Cheeta 45
Cher 299
The Chi Chi Club 177, 206, 207

Linda Christianson 173
George Christy 151
Harriet Cody 198
Nellie Coffman 197, 205
Kevin Cogan 333
Robert H. Cohn 255
Claudette Colbert 72
Nat "King" Cole 72, 93
William "Buster" Collier, Jr. 168
Colony Bungalows 199
Chuck Connors 329
Jackie Coogan 50
Jackie Cooper 54, 92
Charles Correll 177
Lou Costello 293
Joseph Cotten 294
Gordon Coutts 200
Cheryl Crane 58
Joan Crawford 85, 385
Raymond Cree 385
Bing Crosby 66, 149, 151
Cameron Crowe 182
Homer Curran 124
Tony Curtis 175

D

Lila Damita 221
Frantisek Daniel 308
Billy Daniels, Jr. 46
Billy Daniels, Sr. 52
Bobby Darin 81
William S. Darling 352
Mack David 335
Howard Davidson 285
Marion Davies 205
Beryl Davis 327

E

Bette Davis 89, 386
Joan Davis 183
Sammy Davis, Jr. 113, 386
Johnny Dawson 363
Dennis Day 25
Roy Dean 218
Sandra Dee 81
Deep Well Hotel 246
Lucille Demarest 365
William Demarest 336, 365
Jack Dempsey 185
The Desert Inn 205
Desert Museum 197
Armand Deutsch 35
William Devane 377
Sy Devore 56, 208
Marlene Dietrich 344, 350
Noah Dietrich 168
Walt Disney 309, 330
Robert Dix 243
Edward Dmytryk 314
Horace Dodge 386
The Doll House 85
Rosie Dolly 106
Don the Beachcomber 87
Tommy & Janie Dorsey 95
Donald Wills Douglas, Sr. 109
Kirk Douglas 132, 155
Billie Dove 262
Betsy Duncan 303
Donald Duncan 119, 178
Brad Dunning 220
Don Durant 237
George "Bullets" Durgom 96
Leo Durocher 258

Jeanette Edris 90
William Edris 16, 21,
Dwight Eisenhower 386
El Mirador Hotel 138
Arthur Elrod 353
Joey English 284
George Englund 341
Carmene Ennis 365
Maurice Enos 156

F

Davis Factor 102
Jerome Factor 317
Max Factor, Jr. 249
Charlie Farrell 32, 159, 386
Alice Faye 386
Don Fedderson 322
Phil Feldman 56
Mickey Finn 141
Eddie Fisher 318
Irving Florsheim 167
Errol Flynn 176
Gerald & Betty Ford 378
Tennessee Ernie Ford 309
Brian Foy 131, 274
Alan Freed 43
Muriel Fulton 108
Annette Funicello 386

G

Clark Gable 113, 288, 386
Eva Gabor 273, 275
Jolie Gabor 211, 282
Magda Gabor 22
Zsa Zsa Gabor 18, 282, 386
Gant Gaither 146

Palm Springs Celebrity Homes

James Galanos 101
Sergio Galindo 66
Greta Garbo 38, 386
Ava Gardner 143
Erle Stanley Gardner 349
William Gargan 122, 197
Judy Garland 116, 143
Bill & Melinda Gates 378
Gregory Gaye 185
Janet Gaynor 387
Larry Gelbart 325
Harry Gerstad 364
Lawrence Mario Giannini 296
Hoot Gibson 123
Edward Giddings 355
A Arnold Gillespie 229
King Camp Gillette 301
Walter Glatter 108
William Goetz 164
Harper Goff 235, 333
Menahem Golan 218
Samuel Goldwyn 115
Bill Goodwin 297
Frank Gorshin 231
Alex Gottlieb 47
Fred Gottschalk 309
Edmund Goulding 116, 161,
286, 287, 288, 289, 303
Betty Grable 159
Ludovica Dimon Graham 107
B. Donald Bud Grant 288
Cary Grant 171, 179, 345
Shauna Grant 37
Bonita Granville 258
Dorothy Gray 86
Shecky Green 332
Merv Griffin 387

Paul Grimm 223
Werner Groebli 259
Ted Grouya 232
Harry Guardino 233
Val & Yolanda Guest 315

H

Larry Hagman 75
Alexander Hall 35
Monty Hall 323
Alan Hamel 281
Bill Hamilton 150
George Hamilton 88, 136, 150
Harry Hanbury 179
Robert Hanson 113
Jean Harlow 80
Richard Harrison 145
Dorothy Hart 318
Moss Hart 143
Teddy Hart 170, 314, 318
Eden Hartford 183
Don Hartman 261
Laurence Harvey 120
Howard Hawks 105
Goldie Hawn 134, 380
Bill Hay 224
Dick Haymes 154
Louis Hayward 302
Rita Hayworth 300
George Hearst 110
Rosalie Hearst 24, 110
Hugh Heffner 387
Horace Heidt 186
Jascha Heifitz 135
Carol Heiss 164
Leif Henie 321
Sonja Henie 321

Paul Henning 350
Katherine Hepburn 84, 132
Jerry Herman 103, 118
Winston Hibler 164
Alvah Hicks 107
Conrad Hilton 238
Scott Holden 352
William Holden 269, 352, 356, 364
Toni Holt 119
Bob Hope 39, 144, 151, 152, 238, 245, 357
Lena Horne 122
Richard Horner 263
Robert Hornstein 33, 85
Cy Howard 80
Robert Howard 131, 185
Howard Manor 185, 187
Huell Howser 234
Rock Hudson 112
Howard Hughes 74, 176, 177, 181
Thomas Hull 273
Jerry Hulse 82
H. Bruce Humberstone 83
Marion Huntington 154
Barbara Hutton 179
Betty Hutton 142, 328

I

Lee Iacocca 387
Ingleside Inn 202
Charles Irwin 202
Jim Isermann 48

J

Reggie Jackson 387

David Janssen 335
Jergens Family 19
George Jessel 296
Herbert F. Johnson, Jr. 88
John H. Johnson 355
Van Johnson 184
Al Jolson 178
Allan Jones 178, 184
Carolyn Jones 126

K

Gabe Kaplan 99
Stubby Kaye 51
Douglas Keeve 57
John F. Kennedy 66, 67, 150
Kirk Kerkorian 91
Sante Kimes 26
Morgana King 36
Henry Kissinger 387
Robert Kline 368
Philip H. & Penelope Knight 378
C.C. Knudsen 309
Korakia Pensione 200
Murray Korda 250
Sidney Korshak 134
Andre Kostelanetz 282
Stanley Kramer 57
Norman Krasna 178
Milton Krasner 316
Ernst KreneK 17
Irving Krick 125
Richard Krisher 336
Nancy Kulp 201

L

Alan Ladd 74, 186, 213

La Fontaine Retreat 26
Hedy Lamarr 153
Fernando Lamas 230
Gil Lambert 192
Jack Lambert 35
Dorothy Lamour 151
Bennie Lane 351
Richard Lane 251
Sidney Lanfield 329
Richard Lang 160
Walter Lang 291
Mario Lanza 89
Laura La Plante 219
Glen A. Larson 125
Jack Latham 135
Peter Lawford 100
Marc Lawrence 16
Irving "Swifty" Lazar 97
Seymour Lazar 116
Francis Lederer 153
Ruta Lee 44, 114
Eddie LeBaron 124, 130
Harper Lee 387
Andrea Leeds 131, 185, 210
Tim & Beverly LeHaye 379
Janet Leigh 175
Charles LeMaire 334
Mervyn LeRoy 34
Sol Lesser 84, 108
Michael "M.C." Levee 316
Henry Levin 51
Christopher Lewis 147
Jerry Lewis 264
George Liberace 98
Wladziu Liberace 82, 107, 108, 233, 271
Robert Lippert, Jr. 234

Robert Lippert, Sr. 92, 276
Robert Livingston 267
Frank Lloyd 290
Harold Lloyd 172
James Darcie Lloyd 114
Frederick Loewe 24
Raymond Loewy 23
Carole Lombard 113, 386
Julie London 272
Lone Palm Hotel 186, 187
Johnny Longden 387
Trini Lopez 71
Wright S. Ludington 281
Paul Lukas 34
Carl Lykken 123
Arthur Lyons 255

M

Ali MacGraw 354
Shirley MacLaine 387
Klara MacNee 129
Patrick MacNee 129, 251
Guy Madison 379
Marjorie Main 267
Barry Manilow 137, 291, 292
Dorothy Manners 79
Andrew Morgan Maree III 235
Rifael Markowitz 283
Brenda Marshall 364
Peter Marshall 379
Dean Martin 61, 99, 245, 344
Mary Martin 75
Tony Martin 111
Groucho Marx 183
Harpo Marx 369
Michael Masser 165
Tom & Anita May 137

Oscar Mayer 268
William McClatchey 160
Pat McCormick 231
Marie McDonald 263
Maurice McDonald 94
John McEnroe 387
Darren McGavin 44
Rachel McLish 379
Steve McQueen 52, 354
Eric G. Meeks 253, 373
Adolphe Menjou 109
Johnny Mercer 299
Ann Miller 119
Grace Lewis Miller 32
William "Bill" Miller 81
Irving Mills 320
Carmen Miranda 167, 266
Harold Mirisch 73
Marilyn Monroe 66, 95, 150, 168, 205, 387
Reno & Laura Montana 20
Hugo Montenegro 332
George Montgomery 73, 173, 284
Phil Moody 270
Jim Moore 57
Joanna Moore 262
Moorten Botanical Garden 294
Edwin H. Morris 180, 354
Munchkinville 358
George Murphy 309

N
George Nader 112
Tom Neal 15, 85, 144
Jack Nicklaus 387
Andrew Niederman 341, 343

Richard Nixon 387
Greg Niemann 121
Kim Novak 111

O
Donald O'Connor 103, 104
Christina Onassis
Victor Orsatti 263
Ozzy & Sharon Osbourne 379
Reginald Owen 295

P
Patti Page 380
Arnold & Winifred Palmer 380
"Colonel" Tom Parker 105
Eleanor Parker 331
Fess Parker 334
Jay Paley 178
Harriet Parsons 236, 250
John Payne 47
William Pearlberg 171, 174
Joan Perry 170
John Phillips 128, 172
Mary Pickford 88
William H. Pine 266
The Plaza Theatre 204
Hal Polaire 48
Ben Pollack 142, 149
Bob & Eileen "Mike" Pollock 89
Lily Pons 282
Paul Pospesil 286
William & "Mousie" Powell 129
Milton Prell 106
Elvis Presley 19, 56, 75, 77, 105, 208
William Gray Purcell 256

Palm Springs Celebrity Homes

R

The Racquet Club 31
Martin Ragaway 217
Marjorie Rambeau 146
George Randolph 24
Robert Randolph 217
Roy Randolph 150
Donna Reed 71
Billy Reeds 27
Della Reese 220
Phil Regan 98, 179
Nicolai Remisoff 353
Debbie Reynolds 49, 127, 318
Riviera Resort 59
Anne Rice 387
Buddy Rich 83
Herman Ridder 203
John-Paul Riva 350
Maria Riva 343
Jilly Rizzo 225
Anthony Robbins 380
Harold Robbins 90, 110
George Roberson 203
Ronnie Robertson 169
Edward G. Robinson 91
Robinsons Palm Springs 212
Winthrop Rockefeller 133
Buddy Rogers 88, 380
Ginger Rogers 388
Kenny Rogers 388
Tristan Rogers 26
Will Rogers 388
Eleanor Roosevelt 128
Helen Rose 320
George Rosenthal 120
Lillian Roth 368
Irwin Rubenstein 293, 343
Kurt Russell 134, 380
Peggy Ryan 79
Roman Ryterband 145

S

Albert Salmi 49
Ron Samuels 379
Sheppard Sanders 236
Paul Sawtell 244
Joseph Schenck 163
John Schlesinger 342
Dr. William Scholl 255
Irwin Schuman 72, 206
Fred Scott 237
Randolph Scott 388
Frank Scully 229
William A. Seiter 260
Steve Sekely 129
Richard Selzer 50
David O. Selznick 179
Stephen Shagan 80, 130
Sidney Sheldon 94, 131, 132, 133
Lew Sherrell 78
Gregg Sherwood 112
Frank Shields 37
Dinah Shore 73, 173, 388
Sammy Shore 126
Ginny Simms 252, 321
Barbara Sinatra 381
Frank Sinatra 143, 178, 186, 193, 225, 245, 381
Red Skelton 381
Frank Skinner 274
Edward Small 37
Keely Smith 158, 335
Smoke Tree Ranch 309, 337

Index

Smoke Tree Stables 304
Suzanne Somers 281
Spanish Inn 186
Milton Sperling 165
Leo Spitz 117, 128
Robert Stack 298
John M. Stahl 224
Anita Stewart 287
Clifford Stine 55
Milburn Stone 53
George & Ethel Strebe 85
Barbra Sreisand 388
Lynne Stuart 263
Sunset Tower Apartments 104
Robert Surtees 93
A. Edward Sutherland 307
Gloria Swanson 154
Joe Swerling, Jr. 373

T
Akim Tamiroff 221
Sharon Tate 254
Louis Taubman 77
Norman Taurog 162
Elizabeth Taylor 117, 388
Rod Taylor 21, 120
Ruth Taylor 101
Terra Cotta Inn 66
Marlo Thomas 388
Peter M. Thompson 313
Richard Thorpe 269
Kenneth Tobey 265
Michael Todd 117
Norman Tokar 182
Sid Tomack 65
Lily Tomlin 121
Ivan Tors 55

Don Tosti 249
Leo Tover 55
Spencer Tracy 62, 84, 132
Henry Travers 148
John Scott Trotter 166
Paul Troesdale 261, 309
Lana Turner 58

U
Sam Untermeyer 204

V
Elayne Valdez 150
Miguelito Valdez 150, 161
Rudy Vallee 128
Frankie Valli 20
Grace Vanderbilt 349
Jimmy Van Heusen 36
Billy Vaughn 60
Anthony Veiller 264, 265
Villa Royale 270

W
Russell Wade 222, 252
Ralph Waite 381
Robert Wagner 301, 388
Raoul Walsh 145
Charles Walters 136
Joseph & Dee Wambaugh 382
Warm Sands Villas 214
Barbara Warner 80
Harry Warner 127
Jack L. Warner 130, 285, 388
Dale Wasserman 173
Lew Wasserman 115
Nina Wayne 269
Jack Webb 272

James R. Webb 319
Jerry Weintraub 290
Harry Weiss 97
Lawrence Welk 157
Dan Westfall 45
James Whale 201
Paul Whiteman 73
Dick Whittinghill 152
Richard Whorf 254
Michelle Wie 388
Henry Wilcoxon 222
Stephen H. Willard 295
Cindy Williams 78
Fred "The Hammer"
Williamson 327
Beverly Wills 337
Don Wilson 363
Charles Winninger 253
Donald Woods(actor) 319
Donald Woods(producer) 175
Herman Wouk 301
William Wyler 260
Jane Wyman 33, 117

Y

Loretta Young 271
Ralph Young 315

Z

Frank Zane 171
Darryl F. Zanuck 163
Susan Zanuck 307
Paul Zastupnevich 382
Sam Zimbalist 259
Frances Zuchowski 107

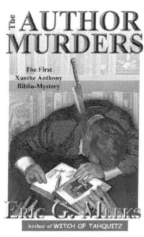

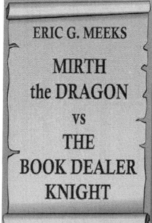

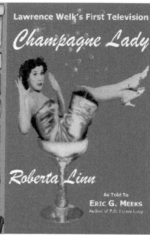

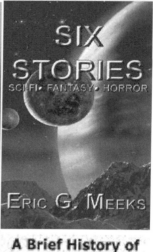

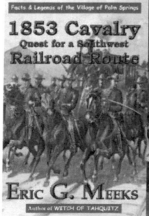